ARTISTRY AND FAITH IN THE BOOK OF JUDITH

SOCIETY
OF BIBLICAL
LITERATURE

DISSERTATION SERIES

Robert R. Wilson, Editor

Number 70
ARTISTRY AND FAITH IN THE BOOK OF JUDITH

by
Toni Craven

Toni Craven

ARTISTRY AND FAITH
IN THE BOOK OF JUDITH

Scholars Press
Chico, California

ARTISTRY AND FAITH IN THE BOOK OF JUDITH
Toni Craven

Ph.D., 1980
Vanderbilt University

Advisor:
Walter Harrelson

Library of Congress Cataloging in Publication Data

Craven, Toni.
　Artistry and faith in the Book of Judith.

　(Dissertation series / Society of Biblical Literature no. 70)
　Bibliography: p.
　1. Bible. O. T. Apocrypha. Judith—Criticism, interpretation, etc. I. Title. II. Series: Dissertation series (Society of Biblical Literature) ; no. 70.
BS1735.2.C73　1983　　229'.24066　　　　　82–25000
ISBN 0–89130–612–9

Printed in the United States of America

To
Walter Harrelson
Distinguished Professor of Old Testament
Vanderbilt University

Contents

Acknowledgments

Final production of this manuscript was funded by generous grants from Brite Divinity School and Texas Christian University. Indices were prepared by Brite Divinity School student Robin T. Black-Dunigan.

I

The Book of Judith:
An Introduction

> Do you happen to know anything about Judith yourself, except
> that she cut off Holofernes' head; and has been made the high
> light of about a million vile pictures ever since, in which the
> painters thought they could surely attract the public to the
> double show of an execution, and a pretty woman, especially
> with the added pleasure of hinting at previously ignoble sin?
>
> —Ruskin[1]

The apocryphal Book of Judith has stimulated an almost countless
number of imaginative responses. Paintings, poems, playing cards, operas,
midrashim, and scholarly publications have taken as their subject the story
of Judith and her exploits.[2] Her story, like her name which literally means
"Jewess,"[3] has a universal quality to it. Purdie rightly says that the story of
Judith has two of the essentials of a great tale: dramatic moments and a

---

[1]John Ruskin, *Mornings in Florence: Being Simple Studies of Christian
Art for English Travellers* (New York: John Wiley & Sons, 1877) 53.

[2]On artistic parallels to the Book of Judith, see Edna Purdie, *The Story
of Judith in German and English Literature* (Paris: Librarie Ancienne Honoré
Champion, 1927), and Bathja Bayer, "The Book of Judith in the Arts," *Ency-
clopaedia Judaica* (10.453-461). On Judith's role in the card-board court, see
Jules R. Block, "Fast Shuffle," *American Way* 12:8 (August 1979) 91-97. See
also, W. Gurney Benham, *Playing Cards* (London: Spring Books, n.d.) 80-81.
From the 1300s on, the Queen of Hearts in the French deck has been
Judith. She was chosen because heart meant courage and because Uzziah
speaks of her good heart and says that the disposition of her heart is good
(Jdt 8:28-29).

[3]There are only two women named Judith in scripture: Judith, the
Hittite wife of Esau (Gen 26:34); and Judith, the pious widow of Bethulia.

great idea.[4] "If number and variety of versions, widespread and enduring popularity, be any criterion of greatness, the tale of Judith, it must be conceded, is one of the great stories of the world's literature."[5]

The Book of Judith is not only an outstanding literary composition but also a profoundly edifying story of faith.[6] On a psychological level,[7] the story invites projections and identifications. Judith lives in a community whose behavior falls short of its ideals; she lives with a people who care deeply about their tradition, but who are so frightened that they convince themselves that they must do anything to survive. In the face of a life-threatening situation, her people are ready to be unfaithful (cf. Jdt 7:27). By contrast, Judith adopts the radical stance that to God alone belongs the decision regarding their survival (8:15). From a position of uncompromising faith, Judith finds a way to cope successfully with the forces that threaten her community. In her triumph, all who are frightened or threatened can participate in the strength and the courage of her orientation to life.

Judith's success is grounded in her trust in Yahweh. On a theological level, her story challenges all who would imprison God in doctrines of their own making. She is faithful to her tradition and to its regulations, but at the same time she is free to act as the circumstances of her particular situation dictate. She demands that her frightened community not put themselves in the place of God. She declares unequivocally that God must be free either to defend them or to witness their destruction. Her confidence is that God will provide, but only her faith assures her of this.

---

[4]Purdie, *The Story of Judith*, 23.

[5]Ibid.

[6]Donald E. Gowan describes both Tobit and Judith as "edifying stories." See his discussion in *Bridge Between the Testaments: A Reappraisal of Judaism from the Exile to the Birth of Christianity* (Pittsburgh: Pickwick, 1976) 353-55.

[7]Jungian psychology, in particular, takes seriously the reading of imaginative literature as a way of exploring the relationship between the feminine and masculine parts of a personality. In speaking of female heroes in stories, Marie-Louise von Franz says, "A feminine figure in a fairy tale with the whole story circling around it does not necessarily prove that the tale has to do with woman's psychology. Many long stories of the sufferings of a woman have been written by men and are projections of their anima problem" (*The Feminine in Fairytales* [Zurich: Spring Publications, 1972] 1). Cf. also Ronda Chervin and Mary Neill, *The Woman's Tale: A Journal of Inner Exploration* (New York: Seabury, 1980), and Erich Neuman, *Amor and Psyche* (Princeton: Princeton University, 1971).

In his book, *The Female Hero in Folklore and Legend,* Tristram Potter Coffin observes that, "Scholars learn it is what the tale-teller and his audience consider a story to be that defines it."[8] In the case of this biblical narrative, the story has become what the written word and the scholar or artist in her or his study say it is. Interestingly, most artists and biblical scholars have focused on a single aspect of the Book of Judith, namely the triumph of a woman who chopped off the enemy's head.[9] It has been a perpetuated accident of circumstances that for most scholars the real story of Judith is the story of chapters 8-16 of the book.[10] The story-teller designed a narrative in which the woman, Judith, does not appear until chapter 8, but many interpreters have simply ignored a full half of the book by focusing their attention on the murder scene.

---

[8]Tristram Potter Coffin, *The Female Hero in Folklore and Legend* (New York: Simon & Schuster, 1975) 5. If Coffin is right that the making of a legend involves "three truisms: that legend tends to seek out the most distinguished figures available; that once these figures are placed in the plot, adjacent facts and incidents tend to rearrange themselves appropriately; and that time and place distortions are easily effected in those things man recalls without written record" (p. 12), then in a sense what scholars and artists have done is to make a legend out of Judith's gory deed. That there is a written record of chapters 1-7 is probably the only reason these chapters have lasted as part of the story.

[9]As a corrective to not knowing anything about Judith, "except that she cut off Holofernes' head, and has been made the high light of about a million vile pictures ever since," Ruskin (*Mornings in Florence,* 53) instructs his readers to write out certain verses from the Book of Judith. Ironically, he advises those who want to know the real story to begin with chapter 8 (p. 53). This same sort of reading of the Book of Judith is encouraged by Nicholas de Lange, *Apocrypha: Jewish Literature of the Hellenistic Age* (New York: Viking, 1978) 114-28. In this recent attempt to popularize the apocryphal writings, de Lange treats chapters 1-7 of the Book of Judith in one paragraph, but he devotes over thirteen pages to chapters 8-16.

[10]See especially, A. E. Cowley, "The Book of Judith," *The Apocrypha and Pseudepigrapha of the Old Testament* (ed. R. H. Charles; Oxford: Clarendon, 1913) 1:242-67. Cowley described chapters 1-7 of the Book of Judith as "the introduction" and chapters 8-16 as "the story proper" (p. 242). For other evaluations that express this same sentiment, see L. H. Brockington, *A Critical Introduction to the Apocrypha* (London: Gerald Duckworth & Co., 1961) 44; Robert C. Dentan, *The Apocrypha, Bridge of the Testaments* (New York: Seabury, 1964) 56; and J. C. Dancy, *The Shorter Books of the Apocrypha* (Cambridge: Cambridge University, 1972) 67.

The first seven chapters are set entirely in communities where men play all the leading roles. This first half of the book describes acts of military aggression and religious compromise. In these chapters, people manipulate each other with the effect that the strong feel superior and the weak feel afraid. It would be interesting to know why scholars and artists have not been attracted to these chapters and why they have focused their attention on that part of the story which tells of the courageous acts of a woman. It might also be interesting to know why I, a woman, have been particularly attracted by these first chapters. Such questions cannot be answered here, though we shall return to them indirectly in later chapters of this study. Here we must simply grant that the anonymous story-teller constructed a story in which first men and then a single woman occupy center stage in a work which is sixteen chapters in length.

Two important and complementary textual studies of Judith have appeared within the last fifteen years. In 1966, A. M. Dubarle published a comprehensive two-volume study which brought together a discussion of the known Hebrew manuscripts and editions.[11] Included in Dubarle's study are thirteen midrashic texts with French translations,[12] but omitted are discussions of the Greek and Old Latin texts of Judith.[13] A recent work fills in these and other gaps in the textual study of the book. In 1979, Robert Hanhart published two volumes dealing specifically with the Greek text and text history of the Book of Judith. One of Hanhart's volumes, as part of the Göttingen Septuagint series, contains the full Greek text together with comprehensive annotation drawn from his study of the various Greek, Old Latin, Vulgate, Syriac, Coptic, Ethiopic, and Armenian textual witnesses.[14] His other volume presents a discussion of these various text forms and the criteria he uses in determining what he calls "der ursprüngliche Text."[15]

---

[11]A. M. Dubarle, *Judith: Formes et Sens des Diverses Traditions*, Tome I: *Études*, Tome II: *Textes* (Rome: Institut Biblique Pontifical, 1966).

[12]Not one of the midrashic texts includes chapters 1-7 of the canonical Greek story. All do include a proposal of marriage for Judith in the enemy camp, and all but one explain her nightly baths outside the enemy camp on the pretext of ritual purification of menstrual uncleanness. These details are not part of the canonical story.

[13]For further comment, see Patrick W. Skehan, "Review of A. M. Dubarle, O.P., *Judith: Formes et sens des diverses traditions, Tome I: Etudes, Tome II: Textes,*" *CBQ* 28 (1966) 347-49.

[14]Robert Hanhart, ed., *Iudith*, in *Septuaginta*, Vol. 8:4 (Göttingen: Vandenhoeck & Ruprecht, 1979).

[15]Robert Hanhart, *Text und Textgeschichte des Buches Judith* (Göttingen: Vandenhoeck & Ruprecht, 1979).

The Greek text exists in three recensions represented by (1) the LXX codices B, א, A and many minuscules; (2) the minuscules 19 and 108 (labeled b' and b, respectively); and (3) the minuscule 58, which is close to the Old Latin and Syriac versions.[16] The LXX codices B, א, A are considered the basic texts. Hanhart prefers the text of B,[17] which is also reproduced in the Cambridge Septuagint. Rahlfs, whose text is followed in this dissertation, follows א more closely.

Because the Greek of B, א, A is replete with Hebraisms such as a regular use of καί for the waw-consecutive, ἐν for ב, πρόσωπον for לפני, and many other idioms, a Hebrew original is posited for the Book of Judith. Jerome claimed a "Chaldee" original for his translation, and though no Hebrew or Aramaic texts for the Book of Judith are now in existence, they are regularly assumed in the text history of Judith. A now non-existent Hebrew original is assumed as the basis of the Greek translation, which in turn served as the basis of the later Aramaic, Hebrew, Old Latin, Syriac, and other translations. Jerome's paraphrastic Vulgate translation, which differs from the Greek version in both its shorter length and its addition and deletion of details, is purported to have been translated from a Chaldee original.[18] I am no longer convinced that we should assume a Hebrew original on the basis of Hebraisms in the Greek text and Jerome's dubious claims.[19] Though the Greek canonical text is structured on Hebrew compositional patterns, it seems equally plausible that the Greek text could have been written from the outset in elegant hebraicised Greek. The author could have been familiar with both the language and the style of "ancient" story-telling. There is, of course, no way to prove these claims, just as there is no way to prove the originality of the non-existent Hebrew and Aramaic texts.

---

[16]For further discussion, see Cowley, "Judith," 244-46; W. O. E. Oesterley, *An Introduction to the Books of the Apocrypha* (New York: Macmillan, 1935) 181; Robert H. Pfeiffer, *History of New Testament Times, With an Introduction to the Apocrypha* (New York: Harper & Brothers, 1949; reprint ed., Westport, Connecticut: Greenwood, 1976) 298; Morton S. Enslin and Solomon Zeitlin, *The Book of Judith* (Leiden: E. J. Brill, 1972) 47; and Hanhart, *Judith*, 11f.

[17]Hanhart, *Judith*, 11f.

[18]For additional discussion, see Enslin and Zeitlin, *Judith*, 45.

[19]For another opinion, see M. Gaster who assumes that the existant medieval Hebrew texts, all of which are abridged modifications of the LXX text, represent the hypothetical original Hebrew. See his study, "An Unknown Hebrew Version of the History of Judith," *Proceedings of the Society of Biblical Archaeology* 16 (1893-94) 156-63. See the discussion of Dubarle, *Judith*, 1:48ff.

It is possible, however, to demonstrate that the Book of Judith, as we now have it in Greek (and in all its sixteen chapters), is structured along the lines of a classical Hebrew narrative with repetition serving as the cornerstone of its composition. It is my contention, though again an unprovable one, that the author included the song of triumph in Judith 16 as a conclusion paralleling the Song of the Sea in Exodus 15 which concludes the exodus story. The following chapters of this study are offered as documentation of the often made claim that the Book of Judith represents one of the best examples of Jewish story-telling.[20]

The following study takes its place among a growing number of studies dedicated to the Book of Judith, three of which deserve special mention. In 1972, two important works on Judith appeared: Morton S. Enslin and Solomon Zeitlin jointly authored a new commentary as part of the Jewish Apocryphal Literature series; and J. C. Dancy published a brief commentary for the text of the New English Bible as a part of the Cambridge Bible Commentary series.[21] In 1974, Alonso-Schökel presented the first paper entirely devoted to a study of the Book of Judith as narrative.[22]

---

[20]As Alonso-Schökel says, "There is a surprising and almost universal agreement among biblical scholars on the literary excellence of this piece of fiction" ("Narrative Structures in the Book of Judith," *Protocol Series of the Colloquies of the Center for Hermeneutical Studies in Hellenistic and Modern Culture*, ed. W. Wuellner, 11:17 [March 1974] 1). Enslin and Zeitlin describe the story as "an example of Jewish Fiction at its best" (*Judith*, 38). Bruce M. Metzger (*An Introduction to the Apocrypha* [New York: Oxford University, 1957] 43) says the book is "one of the best examples of early Jewish story-telling in a setting of warfare." Oesterley claims that "as a literary product the qualities of the book of *Judith* are incontestable" (*Apocrypha*, 175).

[21]Enslin and Zeitlin use Rahlfs' text which tends to follow א (*Judith*, 47). Dancy uses Swete's text which tends to follow B. On the text used in *The New English Bible* which is the translation used by Dancy, see W. D. McHardy, "Introduction to the Apocrypha," *The New English Bible With the Apocrypha* (ed. Samuel Sandmel; New York: Oxford University, 1976) iv.

[22]In speculating on why his is the first wholly literary study of this book, Alonso-Schökel comments, "It is not surprising that there are few literary studies devoted to this book, because biblical scholarship is still reluctant, even hostile, toward such an approach" ("Narrative Structures," 1). Since the publication of his paper in 1975, it seems that biblical critics have become more open to text-centered approaches. In an article entitled "From Analysis to Synthesis: The Interpretation of Genesis 1-11," *JBL* 97 (1978) 23-29, Bernhard W. Anderson addresses what he terms "the

Interestingly, these three works represent not only the best of recent studies on the Book of Judith, but they also reflect the ecumenical character of current scholarship. These three works serve respectively as examples of Jewish, Protestant, and Roman Catholic contributions to the understanding of the literature of the post-exilic period.

Throughout the following study, I will refer to other entries in encyclopedic or introductory works, journal articles, and books that have informed my study of the literary and rhetorical features of Judith. Though I will not present a history of research for the Book of Judith, it is important to note the significance that the canonical status of this story has had in its interpretation. Viewing the book as part of the Apocrypha, many Protestant critics in years past relegated Judith to a second class status. And prior to the publication of Pius XII's encyclical *Divino afflante Spiritu* (1943), Roman Catholic critics defended the deutero-canonical text of Judith as historical.[23]

Special turning points in the study of the Book of Judith trace themselves to three relatively recent works: (1) R. H. Charles, *Apocrypha and Pseudepigrapha of the Old Testament* (1914); (2) C. C. Torrey, *The Apocryphal Literature* (1945); and (3) Robert H. Pfeiffer, *History of New Testament Times* (1945).[24] Each of these works represents a first in biblical scholarship, and each has had a lasting effect on the study of Judith. Charles published the first comprehensive serious commentary on the books of the Apocrypha and Pseudepigrapha.[25] Included in Charles' collection are

---

methodological crisis in which we find ourselves" (p. 23) and concludes that wholly genetic studies are becoming a thing of the past. "If I am not mistaken, a new generation of biblical scholars has arisen that wants to move beyond this kind of analysis to some sort of synthesis, beyond a method that is rigidly diachronic to one that gives appropriate weight to the synchronic dimension of the text" (p. 24).

[23]See "Editors' Preface" to *JBC* (ed. Raymond E. Brown, Joseph A. Fitzmyer, and Roland E. Murphy; Englewood Cliffs: Prentice-Hall, 1968) xvii. On the influence of *Divino afflante Spiritu* on study of the Book of Judith, see Patrick W. Skehan, "Why Leave Out Judith?" *CBQ* 24 (1962) 147-54.

[24]For the full citations for Charles and Pfeiffer, see nn. 10, 16, respectively. See Charles Cutler Torrey, *The Apocryphal Literature: A Brief Introduction* (New Haven: Yale University, 1945).

[25]In the "Preface" to his *The Books of the Apocrypha: Their Origin, Teaching and Contents* (New York: Fleming H. Revell Company, 1914), W. O. E. Oesterley speaks of two important signs of increasing interest in the Apocrypha and Pseudepigrapha in the time just prior to the publication

A. E. Cowley's translation and introduction to Judith.[26] In this important study, Cowley puts forward two arguments that have persisted in almost all subsequent studies of the Book of Judith: (1) he argues that the Book of Judith is "out of proportion" because of an overly long introduction (Judith 1-7) to the "story proper" (Judith 8-16),[27] and (2) he maintains that the Book of Judith represents a Pharisaic point of view.[28] Torrey's study is the first "concise handbook"[29] on the books of the Apocrypha. Of special note in his analysis is his alignment of Bethulia with Shechem.[30] Though this alignment has not been widely endorsed, other studies have also sought to validate the geography of the Book of Judith. Pfeiffer's work is the first which extended an introduction to the Old Testament to include the Apocrypha and Pseudepigrapha. Written as a sequel to his earlier introduction, his study remains one of the most comprehensive treatments of the history and literature of post-exilic Judaism.[31] He argues persuasively that Judith is historical

---

of his study. One is the establishment of the "International Society for the Promoting of the Study of the Apocrypha," and the other is the publication of Charles' "two sumptuous volumes" (p. v). Oesterley says of these volumes that, "this is the most elaborate thing of the kind ever published in any country" (p. vi).

In his own "Preface," Charles notes that Kautzsch published a smaller scale collection of the Apocrypha and Pseudepigrapha in 1900 (*The Apocrypha and Pseudepigrapha of the Old Testament*, iii, n. 1). The Kautzsch volume makes no serious attempt at commentary. Cf. M. Löhr, "Das Buch Judith," in *Die Apocryphen und Pseudepigraphen des Alten Testaments* (ed. E. Kautzsch; Tübingen: J. C. B. Mohr, 1900) 147-64. Following a brief two-page introduction, Löhr presents a German translation of Judith.

[26]See above, p. 5, n. 10.

[27]Cowley, "Judith," 242.

[28]Ibid., 247.

[29]In the "Preface" to his study, Torrey points out that at the time of his writing there was need for a brief introduction to the Apocrypha and the Pseudepigrapha. Of his own work, he says: "There is at present nothing answering to this description either in this country or in Great Britain, and the present volume is an attempt to meet the need" (*The Apocryphal Literature*, v).

[30]Ibid., 91.

[31]In a "Foreword" to his *New Testament Times*, Pfeiffer states that his volume grew out of classes he taught on "The Intertestamental Period" at Boston University School of Theology. He points out that prior to its publication only "the five-volume antiquated English translation of Emil Schurer's great *Geschichte des Judischen Volkes*" was available as a textbook, and it was out of print (p. xi). He describes his work as doing two

fiction.[32] He begins to soften Cowley's description of the work as Pharisaic,[33] but endorses Torrey's identification of Bethulia with Shechem.[34]

In the following chapters, I will treat the Book of Judith as the product of the story-teller's imagination. The focus of this dissertation is the story as story. In working almost exclusively with the Greek text, I have been greatly aided in the final preparation of this dissertation by a computer generated concordance of Judith from the Rahlfs' ninth edition text (Württembergische Bibelanstalt, Stuttgart, 1971) prepared by Richard Edwards.[35]

In Chapter III and Chapter IV of this dissertation, I will demonstrate that the Book of Judith is entirely deserving of the high praise it has received for its literary artistry. On compositional grounds, I will argue that Judith 1-7 is not a faulty introduction to the story proper, but rather a full half of the real story. In Chapter V, as part of my final remarks on the artistry and faith of the Book of Judith, I shall consider the validity of the often made claim that this story represents a Pharisaic orientation to life.

---

things of importance: (1) providing a brief summary of the history, religion, and literature of Judaism from 200 B.C.E. to 200 A.D., and (2) providing a more detailed introduction to the Apocrypha than any other known to him (ibid.).

[32]Ibid., 297.

[33]Ibid., 302. His exact statement is as follows: "To say with Cowley (in Charles, *Apocrypha*, 247) that she was 'a perfect type of Pharisaic righteousness' seems to be too severe an indictment of the Pharisees" (ibid.).

[34]Ibid., 297, n. 15.

[35]The entire Septuagint is available as a whole or in part on machine-readable tape from the *Thesaurus Linguae Graecae Project* at the University of California, Irvine, California. Richard Edwards of Marquette University, Milwaukee, Wisconsin, programmed the concordance used in this dissertation.

II

Methodological Orientation

Current studies of the Book of Judith are for the most part commentaries, studies of the text and its versions, or studies that use a particular set of data drawn from the story as a springboard to an historical discussion of an aspect of post-exilic Judaism.[1] Departing from the focus of these important studies, this dissertation centers on the more narrow concern of describing the literary composition of the Book of Judith. To attempt a study of this sort is to enter waters that are relatively unchartered not only for the Book of Judith, but also for biblical studies in general. This chapter is a statement of the particular orientation and method that will be followed in the subsequent chapters.[2]

ISSUES IN TEXT-CENTERED CRITICISM

The only other wholly literary study of the Book of Judith is that of Alonso-Schökel. His twenty-page paper on "Narrative Structures in the Book

---

[1]For examples of commentaries and textual studies, see above, pp. 4-9, passim. For examples of studies that draw historical discussions from certain aspects of the story, see especially Gottfried Brunner, *Der Nabuchodonosor des Buches Judith: Beitrag zur Geschichte Israel nach dem Exile und des ersten Regierungsjahres Darius I* (Berlin: F. A. Günter & Sohn, 1959), and Hugo Mantel, חסידות קדומה ("Ancient Hasidim"), *Studies in Judaism* (1976) 60-80. Mantel argues that Judith is an important document for understanding the development of the Sadducees.

[2]This chapter is not a fully developed, precise methodological prescription. It is as the title suggests a "methodological orientation" which details the process by which I have formulated the method of my approach in the subsequent chapters.

of Judith" is published in a booklet together with seven responses to it and the minutes of a colloquy devoted to a discussion of these materials at the Berkeley Center for Hermeneutical Studies. In an appendix to his study, Alonso-Schökel says his "is a 'synchronic' analysis at the level of 'speech' (not language)."[3] This method of analysis is "not common in biblical scholarship,"[4] which is more usually concerned with genetic, historical, or theological analysis, he says. His own method of analysis, he avers, is aligned with and indebted to "the masters of New Criticism"—people like Warren and Brooks, H. Hatzfelft and M. Schorer, Lubbock, Foster, and W. Booth.[5]

Two of the respondents take him to task for his methodological claims. Alan Dundes, a professor of anthropology and folklore, points out that the use of the term "structures" in the title of his paper is "so loosely applied as to be virtually without meaning."[6] Dundes himself describes studies of structure as structural delineations of either a syntagmatic or a paradigmatic pattern in a story.[7] Wayne Shumaker, a professor of English literature, takes issue with Alonso-Schökel's claim to use critical methods borrowed from the New Criticism which flourished in the 1940s and 1950s. Shumaker points out that Alonso-Schökel does not assume that Judith is an autonomous literary composition as a good New Critic would, but rather assumes that Judith is a composition in the tradition of Hebrew narratives. So, too, Shumaker argues a New Critic would make much of style, while Alonso-Schökel does not. He concludes, "Finally, I observe, although I do not stress, the fact that since the New Criticism has long ceased to be

---

[3]Alonso-Schökel, "Narrative Structures," 20.

[4]Ibid., 19.

[5]Ibid., 2.

[6]Alan Dundes, "Comment on 'Narrative Structures in the Book of Judith,' " *Protocol Series of the Colloquies of the Center for Hermeneutical Studies in Hellenistic and Modern Culture,* ed. W. Wuellner, 11:17 (March 1974): 27.

[7]Ibid. On the distinction between syntagmatic and paradigmatic structural analysis, Dundes in note 1 refers to the work of Vladimir Propp, *Morphology of the Folktale* (2nd ed.; Austin: University of Texas, 1968) xi-xii. This, in fact, is a reference to Dundes' own introduction to the second edition of Propp's work in which he does in greater detail distinguish syntagmatic structural analysis from paradigmatic structural analysis. Of the first type, he says, "if a tale consists of elements A to Z, the structure of the tale is delineated in terms of this same sequence" (p. xi). And of the second type, he says, "the elements are taken out of a 'given' order and are regrouped in one or more analytic schema" (p. xi).

propagated as such and, indeed, is rarely mentioned by current critics and teachers the adoption of its methods at so late a date might be thought odd."[8]

It should be understood that Alonso-Schökel is taken to task by his critics for his methodological claims, not for his findings. All seven respondents agree that his study is a praiseworthy and "persuasive example of why a literary approach is necessary for a fuller understanding of biblical narratives."[9] It includes a discussion of the Book of Judith under the following five headings: composition, irony, dénouement, characters, and the Book of Judith between celebration and parenesis—a discussion of the function of the story for the Jewish community.

Three issues pertinent to literary study of biblical texts and hence to the methodological orientation of this dissertation emerge from the exchange between Alonso-Schökel and the respondents to his paper: (1) the focus of a synchronic study, (2) the meaning of "structure" in biblical study, and (3) the relationship between the study of a biblical composition and literary criticism.

Recently, categories like synchronic/diachronic[10] or teleological/ genetic[11] have been employed by biblical critics like Alonso-Schökel who attempt something unorthodox in terms of the usual approaches to biblical analysis and who want to describe their enterprise in language which will both distinguish and legitimate it. The main difference between the newer approaches—the synchronic or teleological studies—and the more traditional aproaches—the diachronic or genetic studies—is the function assigned to the

---

[8]Wayne Shumaker, "Critique of Luis Alonso-Schökel on Judith," *Protocol Series of the Colloquies of the Center for Hermeneutical Studies in Hellenistic and Modern Culture*, ed. W. Wuellner, 11:17 (March 1974) 30.

[9]See Dundes, "Comment on 'Narrative Structures in the Book of Judith,'" 27.

[10]According to Daniel Patte (*What is Structural Exegesis?* [Philadelphia: Fortress, 1976] 13, n. 17), the terms synchronic/diachronic are terms proposed by Ferdinand de Saussure to distinguish approaches to linguistic studies, yet in biblical parlance we use the terms to designate various orientations to the text.

[11]Martin Kessler ("Rhetorical Criticism of Genesis 7," *Rhetorical Criticism: Essays in Honor of James Muilenburg* [ed. Jared J. Jackson and Martin Kessler; Pittsburgh: Pickwick, 1974] 1, n. 1) says that the terms genetic/teleological are Northrop Frye's. Kessler does not specify where he has found the terms genetic/teleological in Frye's work.

text.[12] In synchronic or teleological criticism, focus is upon the text itself as the primary generator of critical data. The text itself is "the normative center"[13] of interpretation. By contrast, in diachronic or genetic criticism emphasis includes a set of concerns outside the text. So for instance, source criticism seeks written sources behind the biblical texts, form criticism seeks oral patterns common to given sets of documents, and traditio-historical criticism seeks cross-sectional similarities throughout a body of literature. In these traditional branches of criticism, form and content are subject to a measure of separation as validation of interpretation is sought behind, beyond, or throughout other parallels to a given text.

These distinctions are helpful, but they are not without their own limitations. The terms synchronic/diachronic and teleological/genetic are borrowed from the language of modern linguistic studies. Though the terms can be applied *mutatis mutandis* to distinguish two distinct thrusts in biblical criticism, in practical usage they do little more than broadly describe a critical orientation which is either wholly text-centered or is not. Clarity of communication might well be better served by simply saying a particular study will be text-centered. Since the terms synchronic/diachronic and teleological/genetic do not prescribe a precise methodological stance, it seems an unnecessary multiplication of jargon to adopt the usage of these terms in this dissertation.

---

[12]A notable exception to this generally accepted distinction can be seen in Gottwald's interpretation of the categories synchronics and diachronics. He defines the words parenthetically in a sentence distinguishing the thrusts of historical method from sociological method: "Sociological study of ancient Israel aims at grasping the typical patterns of human relations in their structure and function, both at a given moment or stage (synchronics) and their trajectories of change over specified time spans (diachronics)." He then makes a further distinction that, "historical method embraces all the methods of inquiry drawn from the humanities (e.g. literary criticism, form criticism, tradition history, rhetorical criticism, redaction criticism, history, history of religion, biblical theology)." Gottwald has transposed the linguistic terms synchronic/diachronic to a sociological discussion. In a sense he has done for sociology what other of his colleagues have done in making the text-centered distinction in biblical approaches. Both borrow the terms. See Norman K. Gottwald, "Sociological Method in the Study of Ancient Israel," *Encounter with the Text: Form and History in the Hebrew Bible* (ed. Martin J. Buss; Philadelphia: Fortress, 1979) 69; cf. also 80.

[13]J. P. Fokkelman, *Narrative Art in Genesis* (Assen/Amsterdam: Van Gorcum, 1975) 1.

Alan Dundes's criticism of Alonso-Schökel's use of the word "structures" in the title of the paper "Narrative Structures in the Book of Judith" presents an important issue for text-centered biblical criticism. Indeed, the problem in biblical criticism is larger than the one Dundes presumes when he faults Alonso-Schökel for not using the word "structures" in a paradigmatic or syntagmatic way.[14]   Dundes is speaking out of his structuralist orientation which assumes that a paradigmatic reading is a "vertical" reading and that a syntagmatic reading is a "horizontal" reading.[15]   Both of these terms describe the narrative hierarchy or structural pattern of a text, but in biblical criticism the word "structure" can imply more than a narrative hierarchy.   In fact, Alonso-Schökel defends his use of the word by citing Wellek and Warren's position that a literary work is a system of "structures."[16]

---

[14]For Dundes a *structural* study of a narrative is synonymous with a *structuralist* study.   He offers the following remarks about Alonso-Schökel's use of the word structure in the title of his article on Judith: "I cannot see how discussion of such features as irony or characters in any way constitute a *structural study* of the book of Judith.   If one were serious about attempting a structural study of the story of Judith, one would need to delineate either a syntagmatic pattern (e.g., as in the manner of Propp) or a paradigmatic pattern (e.g., as in the manner of Levi-Strauss). Accordingly, I find the present title of the essay 'Narrative Structures in the Book of Judith' misleading since neither a syntagmatic nor a paradigmatic analysis is undertaken.   A lip service reference to the writings of several French structuralists with an accompanying brief bibliographic footnote is the nearest Professor Alonso-Schökel comes to structural analysis" ("Comment on 'Narrative Structures in the Book of Judith,' " 27).

[15]Daniel Patte, *Structural Exegesis: From Theory to Practice* (Philadelphia: Fortress, 1978) 131.   On "paradym" see p. 131 and pp. 16-23; on "syntagm" see p. 133 and pp. 23-36.   For comments specifically directed to Old Testament study, see Hugh C. White, "Structural Analysis of the Old Testament Narrative," *Encounter With the Text* (ed. Martin J. Buss; Philadelphia: Fortress, 1979) 45-66. See esp. White's section on A. J. Greimas in which he summarizes how the paradigmatic, binary model used by Levi-Strauss has been integrated with the syntagmatic, diachronic or sequential model of narrative analysis (pp. 52-57).

[16]Alonso-Schökel, "Minutes of the Colloquy of March 11, 1974," in "Narrative Structures," 46.   He refers to Rene Wellek and Austin Warren, *Theory of Literature,* (2nd ed.; New York: Harcourt, 1956), but does not cite a page in their work. I suspect he is referring to p. 141, but there Wellek and Warren do not simply say that a literary work is a system of structures, but rather distinguish aesthetically effective aspects of a literary work from the

According to this line of reasoning, any close study of a literary work might be called a study of the "structure" of that literary work. By extension, any line of biblical inquiry closely attendant to the text itself can legitimately appropriate the word "structure." This, of course, results in considerable confusion.

In *Encounter With the Text: Form and History in the Hebrew Bible*, Martin Buss speaks directly to this issue when he says:

> An object does indeed exhibit a structure in the sense that its parts—however defined—truly stand in certain relationships. Yet there are a very large number of ways in which wholes and parts can be identified, and these parts stand in different kinds of relations. Therefore no single structural analysis can lay claim to exclusive validity. Each analysis is relative to the procedures and interests of the observer. In a particular description, one should thus speak not of "the structure," but of "a structure" or of "structures," of an object. A textual study can pay attention to logical relations between content elements, to the sequential arrangement of items (traditionally known as "composition"), to spatial and temporal relations between scenes depicted, to roles of figures in a story, or to a large number of other features.[17]

For the purpose of effective communication, the critic bears the responsibility of defining "structure" for the audience. Thus Dundes is correct in protesting Alonso-Schökel's imprecise use of the word in the title of his paper, but not for the reasons he sets forth. The multidimensional qualities of the word "structure" reflect the multiplicity of approaches to the text as the focal object of analysis. It is to be expected that stylostatics,[18]

---

aesthetically indifferent elements in the following way: " 'Structure' is a concept including both content and form so far as they are organized for aesthetic purposes. The work of art is, then, considered as a whole system of signs, or structure of signs, serving a specific aesthetic purpose."

[17]Martin J. Buss, "The Word as Embracing History and Structure," *Encounter With the Text* (ed. Martin J. Buss; Philadelphia: Fortress, 1979) 9.

[18]For example, see Yehuda T. Radday, "Chiasm in Joshua, Judges and Others," *Linguistica Biblica* 3 (1973) 6-13; Ronald E. Bee, "A Study of Deuteronomy Based on Statistical Properties of the Text," *VT* 29 (1979) 1-22. Cf. also William L. Holladay, "Review of *An Analytical Linguistic Concordance to the Book of Isaiah* (Yehuda T. Radday), *An Analytical Linguistic Key-Word-in-Context Concordance to the Books of Haggai, Zechariah, and Malachi* (Yehuda T. Radday), and *A Synoptic Concordance to Hosea, Amos, Micah* (Francis I. Anderson and A. Dean Forbes)," *JBL* 94:4 (1975) 596.

rhetorical criticism,[19] structuralism,[20] and literary criticism[21] will employ this word variously. Dundes, a folklore structuralist, and Alonso-Schökel, a biblical literary critic, both legitimately use the word, though in entirely different senses. The ambiguity of the term "structure" requires that those who use it make explicit its meaning in their analysis.[22]

Shumaker's criticism of Alonso-Schökel's claimed alignment with New Criticism raises another problem for Alonso-Schökel and for all biblical critics who borrow or adopt the methodologies of English literature critics. It seems that Alonso-Schökel is guilty of a kind of "proof text" citing of New Critics in his paper on Judith. His first comments in the Colloquy are directed to this problem. He says that he meant the alignment of his work with that of the New Critics only as a point of orientation. "If mentioning the New Criticism is disorienting I withdraw it. Any method that first tries to get the meaning through close reading and secondly tries to get the unity

----

[19]See for example, Phyllis Trible, "Wisdom Builds a Poem: The Architecture of Proverbs 1:20-33," *JBL* 94 (1975) 509-18; Anderson, "Interpretation of Genesis 1-11," 23-39. See also Jack R. Lundbom, *Jeremiah: A Study in Ancient Hebrew Rhetoric,* (SBLDS 18; Missoula: Scholars, 1975); and George Rideout, "Prose Compositional Techniques in the Succession Narrative (2 Sam 7, 9-20; 1 Kings 1-2)" Diss., Graduate Theological Union, 1971).

[20]See the essays in *Structuralism: An Interdisciplinary Study* (ed. Susan Wittig; Pittsburgh: Pickwick, 1975). See also the essays in *Encounter With the Text* (ed. Martin J. Buss; Philadelphia: Fortress, 1979), especially those in Part 3, "Structure and History: Linguistic and Literary Studies," 101-34.

[21]See, e.g., the type of analysis proposed by Robert C. Culley, *Studies in the Structure of Hebrew Narrative* (Philadelphia: Fortress, 1976), esp. pp. 69-115. See also the essays in *Semeia* 3 (1975); this entire issue, edited by Robert C. Culley, is devoted to studies in classical Hebrew narrative. For helpful methodological comments, see Charles Conroy, *Absalom Absalom! Narrative and Language in 2 Sam 13-20* (Rome: Biblical Institute, 1978) 1-12. It seems that a scholar like Patrick W. Skehan falls somewhere in between what might be called aesthetic literary criticism and rhetorical criticism. See Skehan's article, "Structure in Poems on Wisdom: Proverbs 8 and Sirach 24," *CBQ* 41 (1979) 365-79.

[22]Even critics claiming the same methodological orientation employ the word "structure" with variety. See, for illustration, the variety of meanings of "structure" in *Rhetorical Criticism: Essays in Honor of James Muilenburg* (ed. Jared J. Jackson and Martin Kessler; Pittsburgh: Pickwick, 1974).

before or beyond the parts, is to the point."[23] He makes the perceptive comment: "Usually the great critics are better at doing criticism than at explaining how they do it."[24]

Charles Conroy's dissertation, *Absalom Absalom*, is an instructive illustration of Alonso-Schökel's two-pronged methodological orientation to the study of the text. Alonso-Schökel was the second reader of the dissertation, and his influence is evident throughout the study, especially in its programmatic design. Part One of Conroy's dissertation is a close reading of the text,[25] while Part Two is an examination of the unity of the text.[26] What Alonso-Schökel and his critics have hammered out in dialogue is described by Conroy as "normal": "A careful reading of any narrative is normally followed by a survey of the text as a whole."[27] Conroy is careful in the way he aligns his work with English literary critics like Wellek and Warren, Lubbock, Brooks, Frye, and others.[28] Conroy, like many other biblical critics, frequently mentions English literary critics in describing his approach to the text, but rarely refers to them in doing his own criticism. He, in fact, frees himself from detailing his indebtedness to English literary critics by saying, "One could engage in endless debate on theoretical questions in literary criticism, but ultimately one must expose oneself to the risk of actually dealing at length with a concrete text."[29] Like Alonso-Schökel he concerns himself with doing criticism rather than explaining how he does it.[30] His adoption of the description "close reading" allows him to approach the text freely not only as the normative center of interpretation, but more

---

[23]Alonso-Schökel, "Minutes of the Colloquy of March 11, 1974," in "Narrative Structures," 45.

[24]Ibid.

[25]Specifically this section is entitled "The Text as Process: Samples of Analytical Close Reading." See Conroy, *Absalom Absalom*, 17-86.

[26]This section is entitled "The Text as Product: A Survey of 2 Sam 13-20 as a Whole." See ibid., 87-145.

[27]Ibid., 87.

[28]Ibid., see esp. his discussion on pp. 6-12.

[29]Ibid., 7.

[30]In the Preface to *Biblical Structuralism: Method and Subjectivity in the Study of Ancient Texts* (Philadelphia: Fortress Press/Scholars Press, 1977), Robert M. Polzin says he wrote his chapter *doing* structural analysis before he wrote his chapter *describing* structural analysis. He adapts what Robert Scholes wrote about artists in *Structuralism in Literature: An Introduction* (New Haven: Yale University, 1974) 9-10, and says "interpretations of their own work by critics are rarely attempted and seldom valuable" (p. v).

importantly as the generator of the very kind of interpretation that will be uncovered. There is, of course, much to be said for this kind of orientation to the text.[31] Alonso-Schökel, Conroy, and most recently Fishbane[32] have adopted the phrase "close reading" to describe their methodological orientation. The phrase will most probably grow in popularity since it states a text centered orientation but promises no specific kind of finding. Like the word "structure," the phrase "close reading" requires elaboration by those who use it. A bow in the direction of English literary critics is not enough. Those who do "close readings" must share with the reader *how* the close reading is to be done.

This point is well made in an exchange between Culley and Tucker.[33] In his article, "Theme and Variation in Three Groups of OT Narratives,"[34] Culley teases that he was tempted to sub-title his article "fiddling around with OT narratives."[35] Culley is in a sense doing a "close reading" of his chosen texts, through what he himself calls an "intuitive operation."[36] Tucker responds to Culley with comments germane to our discussion. Tucker expresses appreciation for the new possibilities for

---

[31]The danger of subjectivity is discussed by Conroy, *Absalom Absalom*, 9.

[32]Michael A. Fishbane, *Text and Texture: Close Readings of Selected Biblical Texts* (New York: Schocken, 1979). For Fishbane, "close reading" is a careful and informed reading of the Bible as a religious teaching whose text is "as Plato would say, the rescued speech" (p. xi) of the meetings between God and humankind. Form and content are inseparable in this reading, though as a literary artifact Scripture requires an interpreter for its renewed life. The "reciprocity between text and reader" (p. xii) is informed by an appreciation of the stylistic structuring of the texts. Fishbane is a sensitive reader, but I feel uneasy about his "close readings" since in texts that I know well, I find that he is often very selective in the details he chooses to highlight. Even though he claims that "the text's meaning is uniquely a function of the active interchange between the reader and what the text continually evokes in him by virtue of its perceived form and style" (p. 8), he also says that "to distinguish between 'objective' facts of form and subjective interpretations of meaning, is singularly misguided" (p. 8). He, in my opinion, performs sensitive close readings, which result in subjective findings of mixed value.

[33]This exchange appears in *Semeia* 3 (1975), "Classical Hebrew Narrative." Culley was editor of this issue.

[34]Robert C. Culley, "Theme and Variations in Three Groups of OT Narrative," *Semeia* 3 (1975) 3-13.

[35]Ibid., 3.

[36]Ibid., 10.

understanding Old Testament narratives that are being opened up by Culley's intuitive insights, but he urges explicit methodological reflection, saying:

> If I and others are to play at Culley's game we must know the rules, or at least be in the process of formulating those rules. Such is the fundamental difference between criticism and whimsey, that it operates more or less self-consciously with one set of rules or another, that it has not only a method but a methodology.[37]

ORIENTATION OF THIS STUDY

Having noted, though even in a limited way, the difficulties attendant on the use of words like synchronic/diachronic and structure and on the adoption of language and methods borrowed from other fields like linguistic analysis or literary criticism, we see the need to set out as clearly as possible the rules that will govern this study of Judith. The primary focus of this study is the story itself. It is a "close reading," of a literary/rhetorical kind, of the "structure" of the Book of Judith. When I use the word "structure" I have in mind something akin to a narrative x-ray of the architectural skeleton or compositional pattern that undergirds the story.

Key to the filling out of this picture of the compositional skeleton of the story will be the discovery of repetitions or correspondences both within each of the halves of the book and between the two halves of the book. I have called these correspondences by four names: (1) expressed identities, (2) expressed antitheses, (3) implied antitheses, and (4) artificial identities. Expressed correspondences are those which contain at least one set of equivalent or identical terms. Implied correspondences are those in which implicitly parallel elements of the story are sharply contrasted with each other. And artificial identities are those in which subtle grammatical or functional correspondences are achieved by skillfully matched components in the story. These terms will be fully explicated in the following chapter of the dissertation. My aim here is simply to state, if I may once again borrow Tucker's words, the rules of my game or my critical orientation, and to share the process out of which I have formulated these categories of correspondence.

I have been particularly influenced by the works of Robert Lowth and James Muilenburg. My methodological orientation is that of literary/ rhetorical criticism, but the particular aspect of the kind of criticism that I

---

[37] Tucker, "Comments on the Articles of Robert C. Culley and Burke O. Long," 146.

here espouse is a type of criticism that might best be called "compositional analysis." It is my intent in the remainder of this chapter to detail my indebtedness to Lowth and most especially to Muilenburg and to show where and how my analysis of the text departs from the orientation of these two scholars.

The Influence of Robert Lowth

The classic study of patterns of repetition in Hebrew poetry is that of Robert Lowth. In the nineteenth lecture in *Praelectiones de Sacra Poesi Hebraeorum* (1753) and again in the introductory remarks in *Isaiah. A New Translation; with a Preliminary Dissertation, and Notes Critical, Philological, and Explanatory* (1778), he describes a phenomenon in Hebrew poetry that he terms *parallelismus membrorum*.[38] The 1753 work on Hebrew poetry, Lowth's first major publication, is the product of his ten years as Professor of Poetry at Oxford (1741-1751). As the title shows, it is written in Latin, the cultured language of his time.[39] The 1778 work on Isaiah, Lowth's last major publication, is the product of his time in various churches as a member of the clergy of the Church of England,[40] and it was published

---

[38]For Lowth's discussion of parallel members, see "Lecture XIX," in *Lectures on the Sacred Poetry of the Hebrews* (trans. from the original Latin by G. Gregory; A New Edition with Notes by Calvin E. Stowe; Boston: Crocker & Brewster, 1829) 154-66. See also, *Isaiah: A New Translation; with a Preliminary Dissertation, and Notes Critical, Philological, and Explanatory* (originally published in 1778; London: W. Baynes and Son, 1825) 15-26.

[39]See Aelred Baker, "Parallelism: England's Contribution to Biblical Studies," *CBQ* 35 (1973) 429-40, for an interesting evaluation of Lowth's work and its antecedents. Baker points out that the Latin style of *Praelectiones* was used by Keble who followed Lowth in the next century to justify the continued use of Latin in the Oxford lecture halls (p. 432, cf. n. 25).

[40]The value Lowth placed on education and especially language study can be seen in the titles of his major publications. In addition to pamphlets and sermons, he published five books: (1) *De Sacra Poesi Hebraeorum* (1753). (2) *The Life of William of Wykeham, Bishop of Winchester* (1748), a work in which he expressed profound thanks for his own education. (3) *A Short Introduction to English Grammar* (1762), a work considered a masterpiece in his own day. In the *Memoirs of the Life and Writings of the Late Right Reverend Robert Lowth, D.D.* (London: W. Bent, 1787) (anonymous), it says of this book that "it is, or ought to be, in the hands of every person, who would write his native tongue with elegance and propriety" (p. 10).

just after his appointment as Bishop of London, the position he occupied until his death.[41] This work, written in English, is a refined restatement and

---

(4) *Isaiah: A New Translation; with a Preliminary Dissertation, and Notes Critical, Philological, and Explanatory* (1779). (5) *Directions for the Profitable Reading of the Holy Scripture*, published shortly after Lowth's death in 1787 this work is actually his father's work which Lowth prepared for publication. It is interesting that Lowth's first and last original publications both dealt with the subject of parallelism.

[41]After Lowth left his Chair of Poetry at Oxford, he made six moves: in 1750 he became archbishop of Winchester; in 1753, rector of Woodhay, Hampshire; in 1775, prebendary of Durham and rector of Sedgefield; in 1766, bishop of St. David's. He moved to Oxford this same year and to the see of London in 1777. He remained in this last position until his death, having declined the Archbishopric of Canterbury in 1783.

His family life was marked by the youthful deaths of five of his seven children. Following the death of his son Thomas-Henry, Bishop Lowth built a family vault in Fulham Church Yard, "thereby intimating his resolution to live and die—Bishop of London" (*Memoirs*, 16). Only his second son, the Rev. Robert Lowth, and his third daughter, Martha Lowth, lived beyond the Bishop's own death.

His eldest and most promising son, Thomas-Henry, died in 1778 when only twenty-five years old. His eldest daughter, Mary, died at thirteen (1768). His second daughter, Frances, died unexpectedly while serving coffee in their Fulham home to Bishop Lowth, his wife, and several of their friends (1783); Frances was twenty-six at the time of her death. His fourth daughter, Margaret, died at six (1769), and his fifth daughter, Charlotte, at three (1768). With the exception of his eldest daughter, Mary, who is buried at Cuddesdon in Oxfordshire, the entire family is buried together in an elegant monument in Fulham Church Yard. There is a handwritten addition to Harvard University's 1787 copy of the *Memoirs* (BR 6312.80, pp. 26f.) that describes the details of the Fulham Church Yard monument.

Mary's epitaph hints at the grave sadness Lowth felt at her death even as it demonstrates how thoroughly he had internalized the repetitions of parallelism:

> Care, vale, ingenio praestans, pietate, pudore,
>   Et plusquam natae nomine cara, vale:
> Cara Maris, vale! ar veniet felicius aevum,
>   Quando iterum tecum, sim modo dignus, ero.
> "Caro, redi," laeta tum voce dicam, "paternos
>   Eja age in amplexus, cara Maria, redi."

The epitaph and the following translation by the Rev. Mr. Dunscombe are found in the *Memoirs*, p. 20. The translation does not capture the rhythm of the Latin parallelism but rather draws its cadence from rhymed

expansion of many of his earlier findings. Baker says, "It was this work that really brought the idea of 'parallelism' to the notice of the general reading public."[42]

In the Isaiah translation, we find his famous words that lines of poetry are in a synonymous relationship when they "correspond one to another by expressing the same sense in different, but equivalent terms; when a proposition is delivered, and is immediately repeated, in the whole or in part, the expression being varied, but the sense entirely, or nearly the same."[43] For example:

> Listen to me,   O coastlands
> and hearken,   you peoples from afar.
> The Lord called me   from the womb
> from the body of my mother   he named my name.
>
>   Isa 49:1

In this illustration of synonymous parallelism, every element has a direct correspondence in the subsequent line. But the fullness of these correspondences and the consecutive arrangement of the lines (a,a,b,b) are not essential for synonymous parallelism as it is defined by Lowth. His own scriptural examples in the Isaiah translation show great variety in both the number of corresponding elements and the arrangement of the synonymous lines.

The corresponding elements of lines in synonymous parallelism can occur at the beginning of lines:

> The waters saw thee, O God;
> The waters saw thee; they were seized with anguish.
>
>   Ps 77:16 (Lowth's translation)[44]

---

last words:
> Dearer than daughter, parallel'd by few.
> In genius, goodness, modesty,—adieu;
> When,—if deserving—I, with thee, shall rest.
> "Come," then thy fire will cry, in joyful strain,
> "O come to my paternal arms again!"

[42]Baker, "Parallelism," 431. He includes an interesting reaction that Sir Joshua Reynolds had after his reading of *Isaiah*. Reynolds saw a similarity between Lowth's study of parallelism and the effect repeated words had on the ear and his own paintings and the effect repeated colors had on the eye. See p. 431, n. 16.

[43]Lowth, *Isaiah*, 15.

[44]Ibid., 17.

Or they can occur at the end of the lines:

> Hearken unto me, O house of Jacob;
> And all the remnant of the house of Israel.
>   Isa 46:3 (Lowth's translation)[45]

The lines can be arranged in consecutive a,a patterns as in the previous two examples, or in alternating a,b,a,b, patterns:

> As the heavens are high above the earth;
>   So high is his goodness over them that fear him.
> As remote as the east is from the west;
>   So far hath he removed from us our transgression.
>   Ps 103:11-12 (Lowth's translation)[46]

Four-line a,a,b,b, sequences are also possible:

> The ox knoweth his possessor;
> And the ass the crib of his lord;
>   But Israel doth not know Me;
>   Neither doth my people consider.
>   Isa 1:3 (Lowth's translation)[47]

So, too, five-line a,a,b,c,c or a,a,b,b,c patterns are cited by Lowth as examples of synonymous parallelism:

> Who is wise, and will understand these things?
> Prudent, and will know them?
>   For right are the ways of Jehovah;
>   And the just shall walk in them;
>   But the disobedient shall fall therein.
>   Hos 14:9 (Lowth's translation)[48]

> Who established the word of his servant;
> And accomplisheth the counsel of his messengers:
>   Who sayeth to Jerusalem, Thou shalt be inhabited:
>   And to the cities of Judah, Ye shall be built;
>   And her desolate places I will restore.
>   Isa 44:26 (Lowth's translation)[49]

---

[45]Ibid., 16.
[46]Ibid., 19.
[47]Ibid., 18.
[48]Ibid., 19.
[49]Ibid.

In sum, Lowth's own examples of synonymous parallelism show both fluidity and variation in the number of correspondences between parallel lines and in the patterns of their arrangement. Examples range from simple two-line illustrations to "elegant,"[50] intricate four and five-line examples.

Lowth's second category of parallelism, antithetic parallelism, also allows for fluidity in the number of terms in opposition and in the patterns of their arrangement. Of this type of parallelism Lowth says:

> The second sort of parallels are the antithetic: when two lines correspond with one another by an opposition of terms and sentiments; when the second is contrasted with the first, sometimes in expressions, sometimes in sense only. Accordingly the degrees of antithesis are various; from an exact contraposition of word to word through the whole sentence, down to a general disparity, with something of a contrariety, in the two propositions.[51]

His examples of antithetic parallelism include couplets in which every term has its opposite:

> A wise son rejoiceth his father;
> But a foolish son is the grief of his mother.
> Prov 10:1 (Lowth's translation)[52]

They also admit four-line a,a,b,b oppositions like the following:

> Yet a little while, and the wicked shall be no more;
> Thou shalt look at his place, and he shall not be found:
> But the meek shall inherit the land,
> And delight themselves in abundant prosperity.
> Ps 37:10-11 (Lowth's translation)[53]

> For the mountains shall be removed;
> And the hills shall be overthrown:
> But my kindness from thee shall not be removed;
> And the covenant of my peace shall not be overthrown.
> Isa 54:10 (Lowth's translation)[54]

---

[50]Lowth favors the word "elegant" in discussing parallelism. See, e.g., *Isaiah*, 20, 21, 23, 26, and *Sacred Poetry of the Hebrews*, 157, 160, 161. Often he seems to use this word to describe how parallelism functions to produce elegant compositions.

[51]Lowth, *Isaiah*, 20.

[52]Ibid.

[53]Ibid., 21.

[54]Ibid., 21-22.

Lowth's third category of parallelism, synthetic or constructive parallelism, is artificial or "author made" parallelism. In this type of parallelism,
he says:

> . . . there are perhaps no two lines corresponding one with
> another as equivalent, or opposite in terms; yet there is a
> parallelism equally apparent, and almost as striking, which
> arises from the similar form and equality of lines, from the
> correspondence of the members and the construction; the con-
> sequence of which is a harmony and rhythm, little inferior in
> effect to that of the two kinds preceding.[55]

Formally, he finds synthetic or constructive parallelism:

> . . . where the parallelism consists only in the similar form of
> construction; in which word does not answer to word, and
> sentence to sentence, as equivalent or opposite; but there is a
> correspondence and equality between different propositions, in
> respect of the shape and turn of the whole sentence, and of the
> constructive parts; such as noun answering to noun, verb to verb,
> member to member, negative to negative, interrogative to
> interrogative.[56]

Because Lowth only cites his examples of parallelism and does not
explain which elements are parallel, his examples of synthetic parallelism
are particularly difficult to interpret. As an illustration of synthetic
parallelism, Lowth cites a fifteen-line call to worship taken from Psalm
148. His translation of the poem suggests that the first twelve lines break
into six two-line units of address that call (1) the inhabitants of the deep,
(2) the elements of nature, (3) growing things and their homes, (4) animals,
(5) earthly rulers, and (6) those who are ruled to praise the name of the
Lord. The last three lines of the poem form an expanded justification for
this imperative to worship which recapitulates the opening words of the
poem, "Praise the Lord." The parallelism in the poem is in its construction
rather than in explicit verbal repetitions.

ADDRESS:

(1)	inhabitants of the deep	⌈ Praise ye Jehovah, ye of the earth; ⌊ Ye sea-monsters, and all deeps:
(2)	elements of nature	⌈ Fire and hail, snow and vapour; ⌊ Stormy wind, executing his command:

---

[55]Ibid., 24.
[56]Ibid., 22.

(3)	growing things and their homes	⌈Mountains, and all hills; ⌊Fruit-trees, and all cedars:
(4)	animals	⌈Wild beasts, and all cattle ⌊Reptiles, and birds of wing;
(5)	earthly rulers	⌈Kings of the earth, and all peoples; ⌊Princes, and all judges of the earth:
(6)	those who are ruled	⌈Youth, and also virgins; ⌊Old men, together with the children:
COMMAND:		⌈Let them praise the name of Jehovah; For his name alone is exalted; ⌊His majesty, above earth and heaven.

Ps 148:7-13 (Lowth's translation)[57]

Lowth states that three-line stanzas are the most common examples of synthetic parallelism.[58] His translation of Ps 135:6-7 illustrates this pattern.

כל אשר-חפץ יהוה עשה בשמים ובארץ בימים וכל-תהומות:

מעלה נשאים מקצה הארץ ברקים למטר עשה מוצא-רוח

1 ⌈Whatsoever Jehovah pleaseth,
2 │That doeth he in the heaven, and in the earth;
3 ⌊In the sea, and in all deeps:
1 ⌈Causing the vapours to descend from the ends of the earth;
2 │Making the lightnings with the rain;
3 ⌊Bringing forth the wind out of his treasures.

Ps 135:6-7 (Lowth's translation) [59]

As an aid to understanding the preceding example, I have numbered the lines in the "three line stanzas" and I have underlined the words in Lowth's translation which correspond to the repeated preposition ב in verse 6 of the Hebrew and to the repeated participial forms in verse 7. The grammatical identities in his translation demonstrate what Lowth meant when he spoke of the striking correspondence of forms of construction in synthetic parallelism. His translation of וכל-תהומות as "in all the deep" (vs. 6) is apparently an emendation, one which interestingly is suggested by several manuscripts in *BHS*.[60]

---

[57]Ibid. Diagrammatic explanation added.

[58]Ibid., 23.

[59]Ibid.

[60]*Biblia Hebraica* (ed. Rudolf Kittel; Stuttgart: Württembergische Bibelanstalt, 1966) 1092, n. 135: 6.

It is appropriate here to note that for Lowth the theory of parallelism provided a set of criteria for the emendation of difficult texts.[61]   In his time, there were no critical texts of versions and Lachmann had not yet shown how to group manuscripts.[62]   Lowth used parallelism "to restrict and control the celebrated 18th century art of emendation."[63]   His objective was to be a faithful translator. As he himself said:

> The first and principal business of a Translator is to give the plain literal and grammatical sense of his author; the obvious meaning of his words, phrases, and sentences, and to express them in the language into which he translates, as far as may be, in equivalent words, phrases, and sentences.[64]

His own training and interest in English grammar, Latin, Greek, and Hebrew equipped him well as a sensitive translator. And it is to his credit that many of the suggestions that he made regarding the translation of portions of the Bible have been widely accepted.[65]   His closing remarks in "Lecture XIX" bespeak his own vision of parallelism as a tool for both translators and commentators:

> But should all that has been remarked concerning the members and divisions of the sentences appear light and trifling to some persons, and utterly undeserving any labour or attention; let them remember that nothing can be of greater avail to the proper understanding of any writer, than a previous acquaintance with both his general character, and the peculiarities of his style and manner of writing: let them recollect that translators and commentators have fallen into errors upon no account more frequently, than for want of attention to this article; and indeed, I scarcely know any subject which promises more copiously to reward the labour of such as are studious of sacred criticism, than this one in particular.[66]

Terrien holds that Lowth's understanding of parallelism "led the way to the   historical   concreteness   which   characterized   biblical   exegesis

[61]See Charles Augustus Briggs, *Biblical Study: Its Principles, Methods and History*(New York: Scribner's, 1891) 203. Cf. also Baker, "Parallelism," 439.

[62]Baker, "Parallelism," 439.

[63]Ibid., 439, n. 48.

[64]Lowth, *Isaiah*, xi.

[65]Baker, "Parallelism," 438-39. See n. 49 for additional literature.

[66]Lowth, *Sacred Poetry of the Hebrews*, 166.

subsequently."[67] It is true that Lowth's realization of the peculiar nature of Hebrew poetry made possible a fuller appreciation of the literature of the Bible. His advice that attention to parallelism could lead to proper understanding and copious rewards in some ways sounds surprisingly contemporary. But neither Lowth nor his English contemporaries fully realized the importance of his discovery for literary criticism.[68] Lowth's most important works, his two studies of parallelism in Hebrew poetry and his introduction to English grammar,[69] show that his primary scholarly interest was to further the responsible use and appreciation of language. Yet the orientation of his work did indeed influence that of many later exegetes, including Herder, Gunkel,[70] Gray,[71] Mowinckel,[72] Muilenburg,[73] and in some sense all who attend seriously to the form or construction of Hebrew literary patterns. While it seems an overstatement for Cheyne to judge Lowth a "vox clamantis in deserto,"[74] it is nonetheless true that it is Lowth whom later biblical exegetes acknowledge and take to task. It is equally true, as Baker has pointed out, that Johann Schoettgen and Mazzocchi were

---

[67] Samuel Terrien, "History of the Interpretation of the Bible," *IB* (ed. George A. Buttrick; New York: Abingdon, 1952) 1.131.

[68] Briggs, *Biblical Study*, 203.

[69] A note prefacing the reprinted edition of Lowth's grammar claims that his grammar was probably the most influential English grammar produced in the eighteenth century. It was the basis for numerous other grammars published between 1763 and 1840, and could claim authority which no other grammar had before Webster. It was published anonymously; Lowth's name appeared only on volumes printed in America and Ireland. Its title perhaps deliberately imitates that of the first part of Lily's celebrated Latin grammar. See *Robert Lowth, A Short Introduction to English Grammar 1762*, in *English Linguistics 1500-1800 (A Collection of Facsimile Reprints)* (Selected and ed. R. C. Alston; Menston, England: The Scolar Press Limited, 1967), 18.

[70] For discussion, see James Muilenburg, "Introduction," in Hermann Gunkel, *The Psalms* (Philadelphia: Fortress, 1967) iv.

[71] See George Buchanan Gray, *The Forms of Hebrew Poetry* (London: Hodder and Stoughton, 1915), reprint ed., with Prolegomenon by D. N. Freedman (n. p.: Ktav, 1972).

[72] See Sigmund Mowinckel, *The Psalms in Israel's Worship* (trans. D. R. Ap-Thomas; New York: Abingdon, 1967) 2.166f.

[73] See James Muilenburg, "A Study in Hebrew Rhetoric: Repetition and Style," *VTSup* (Leiden: E. J. Brill, 1953) 1.97-111.

[74] T. K. Cheyne, *Founders of Old Testament Criticism* (Jerusalem: Raritas, 1971) 3-4, n. 1.

independently on the same track as Lowth in describing the phenomenon in Hebrew poetry and that Lowth was greatly assisted by the understanding of rhetoric in his day.[75]

No aspect of Lowth's work has been more seriously questioned than his statement on synthetic parallelism or, as he alternately called it, constructive parallelism. The notion that this kind of parallelism is not true parallelism, but rather a loosely connected relationship between two lines of poetry in which the second line develops or completes the thought of the first, is widespread[76] and can most likely be traced to George Buchanan Gray. By 1915, Gray had reduced examples of parallelism to two-line couplets and had seriously questioned the legitimacy of synthetic parallelism by saying that two lines in synthetic parallelism "are parallel to one another merely in the way that the continuation of the same straight line is parallel to its beginning."[77] Very early on, Gray's work was judged "the soundest attempt to analyse and classify the various forms that parallelism may take,"[78] and this judgment persists.   D. N. Freedman notes in his

---

[75]Baker, "Parallelism," 433-38, 440. For some additional comment on the question of priority and for a summary of both the life and work of Schoettgen, see Lundbom, *Jeremiah: A Study in Ancient Hebrew Rhetoric,* 121-27. Here Lundbom makes the important point that Lowth did not use Schoettgen's work in formulating his own principles of parallelism even though Briggs and Meek have made statements to that effect. Lundbom also corrects the mistaken notion that Schoettgen was a rabbi when in fact he was a Christian philologist. And finally, he presents for the first time in English Schoettgen's ten canons of "Exergasia Sacra." He concludes by comparing Schoettgen's canons with Lowth's three types of parallelism, and argues that Schoettgen's lists anticipate the later refinements of Lowth by Gray. Gray's terminology "incomplete parallelism without compensation" and "incomplete parallelism with compensation" finds direct parallels in some of Schoettgen's canons.

[76]See, for example, Aage Bentzen, *Introduction to the Old Testament* (Copenhagen: G. E. C. Gad, 1958) 1.119; Otto Eissfeldt, *The Old Testament: An Introduction* (trans. P. R. Ackroyd; New York: Harper & Row, 1974) 57; or Georg Fohrer, *Introduction to the Old Testament* (trans. David E. Green; New York: Abingdon, 1968) 46, for statements of the criticism that synthetic parallelism is not really parallelism but rather a supplemental relationship between two lines in which the second carries forth the idea of the first. All three scholars make this point as a summary of what Lowth said about synthetic parallelism. This is a misrepresentation of Lowth; see above, pp. 23-25, for Lowth's own description of synthetic parallelism.

[77]Gray, *Hebrew Poetry,* 50.

[78]Theodore H. Robinson, *The Poetry of the Old Testament* (London: Duckworth, 1947) 26.

"Prolegomenon" to the 1972 reprinted edition of Gray's work that Gray added "a significant measure of clarity and precision"[79] to the principles of parallelism and that "he exposed the weakness of Lowth's catchall third category, synthetic parallelism."[80]

Gray's explanation of synthetic parallelism is restated in Bentzen's *Introduction to the Old Testament*, although the footnotes do not reflect this dependence. Bentzen's statement that synthetic parallelism is not "real parallelism unless we accept the sophistical explanation that a straight line is parallel to itself"[81] seems too close to Gray's statement to be accidental. Not only has Gray's denigration of synthetic parallelism found wide acceptance among biblical critics, but his multiplication or more properly his subdivision of Lowth's three categories of parallelism has also left its mark. In a recent discussion of parallelism, Thompson says that three other types of parallelism have been proposed to supplement the types set forth by Lowth: emblematic parallelism, stairlike parallelism, and introverted parallelism.[82]

---

[79]"Prolegomenon" by D. N. Freedman, in Gray, *Hebrew Poetry*, xxv.
[80]Ibid.
[81]Bentzen, *Introduction*, 119.
[82]Thomas L. Thompson, *Introducing Biblical Literature: A More Fantastic Country* (Englewood Cliffs: Prentice-Hall, 1978) 19. I cite Thompson here because his recent study is readily available and because it is so clearly presented. The three additional categories he lists, however, are found in E. G. Briggs's *Introduction to the Psalms* (1906) and are listed in T. H. Robinson's *The Poetry of the Old Testament* (1947) 23.
The following is taken from Thompson's discussion of parallelism where after having listed Lowth's three categories, he continues to list these additional types of parallelism:
(d)   emblematic parallelism, in which one of the lines presents as a simile the thought of the other:
>   *As* a hart longs for flowing streams,
>   So longs my soul for thee O God.
>   Ps 42:1
(e)   stairlike parallelism, in which part of one line is repeated in the second, but also developed further:
>   Ascribe to the Lord, O heavenly beings,
>   Ascribe to the Lord glory and strength.
>   Ascribe to the Lord the glory of his name;
>   Worship the Lord in holy array.
>   Ps 21:1-2
(f)   introverted parallelism, in which the members of the lines are in chiastic order:
>   *We have escaped* as a bird from *the snare* of the fowlers;
>   The *snare* is broken, and *we have escaped*.
>   Ps 124:7

To this list we might add climactic parallelism[83] and parabolic paral-lelism.[84] And there are undoubtedly other types that could be added here. In fact, though most scholars accept Lowth's three types of parallelism with reservations about synthetic parallelism, they do not agree on either the definition or number of types of parallelism that should supplement his list.

As an illustration of this problem, let us consider the case of climactic parallelism. Of this type of parallelism, S. R. Driver says, "the first line is itself incomplete, and the second line takes up words from it and completes them."[85] Both he and Mowinckel cite Ps 21:1 as an example of climactic parallelism.[86] In this example, the second half of the verse makes explicit *what* is to be ascribed to the Lord, namely, "glory and strength":

> Ascribe to the Lord, O heavenly beings,
> Ascribe to the Lord glory and strength.

Their example does indeed illustrate the definition they both espouse. However, if I were describing the kind of parallelism found in Psalm 29, I would call it synonymous parallelism following Lowth's original definition, for here a proposition is delivered and then immediately repeated in part in

---

[83]This type will be discussed below.

[84]See Klaus Koch, *The Growth of the Biblical Tradition: The Form-Critical Method* (New York: Scribner's, 1969) 94. Koch maintains that there are five types of parallelism, the last of which is parabolic parallelism in which two lines of poetry make "a comparison in such a way that the image presented in the first row is taken up as the point of the second":

For as the heaven is high above the earth,

So great (high) is his mercy toward them that fear him.

                                   Ps 103:11

Koch's "parabolic parallelism" is Thompson's "emblematic parallelism." See above, n. 82.

[85]S. R. Driver, *An Introduction to the Literature of the Old Testament* (New Edition; New York: Scribner's, 1916) 363.

[86]Ibid.; Mowinckel, *The Psalms in Israel's Worship*, 2.167. Note that Thompson (*Introducing Biblical Literature*) cites Ps 29:1-2 as an example of stairlike parallelism. Briggs (*Biblical Study*) and Robinson (*The Poetry of the Old Testament*) also cite Ps 29:1-2, but as an example of stairlike parallelism. Koch treads a middle way by citing Ps 29:1 as an example of a category he calls an "ancient form" of "stair-like, or climactic, tautological, or repetitive parallelism" (*The Growth of the Biblical Tradition*, p. 94). His underlining suggests that he favors the designation stairlike, but his title of this category with all its possible names is more inclusive.

the repetition of the phrase "ascribe to the Lord." Then I would extend the example to include the following verse so that it reads as follows:

> Ascribe to the Lord, O heavenly beings,
> Ascribe to the Lord glory and strength.
> Ascribe to the Lord the glory of his name;
> Worship the Lord in holy array.

Ps 29:1-2

The synonymous expression הבו ליהוה appears at the beginning of the first three lines of the psalm. Where I would move beyond Lowth's description is that I would say here we have a three-fold synonymous repetition building to a climax in the call to worship the Lord. Using Lowth's descriptive category, I would speak of how this type of parallelism functions in the architecture of the psalm. By distinction, I would say that Driver and Mowinckel describe a figure of parallelism. And this figure is really a sub-division or refinement of Lowth's synonymous parallelism. The repetition of "ascribe to the Lord" at the beginning of each line in verse 9 qualifies this verse as an example of Lowth's synonymous parallelism, and the specification "glory and strength" further qualifies it as an example of Driver's and Mowinckel's climactic parallelism.

Interestingly, Driver's second example of climactic parallelism illustrates this same issue. And since it is drawn from the same psalm as discussed above, it serves to reinforce the distinction I am trying to draw between his description of a figure of parallelism and my use of Lowth's categories to describe a function of parallelism in the compositional texture of the psalm. Driver maintains that the specification in Ps 29:8b of precisely which wilderness the Lord shaketh is an illustration of climactic parallelism:

> The voice of the Lord shaketh the wilderness:
> The Lord shaketh the wilderness of Kadesh.[87]

In Lowth's terminology, this verse would be an example of synonymous parallelism since the words "the Lord shaketh" appear in each line. And since the phrase קול יהוה appears a total of seven times in Psalm 29 (vv 3, twice in 4, 5, 7, 8, 9), I would argue that this seven-fold repetition of synonymously parallel subjects fulfills a function whose discovery enriches our understanding of the meaning of the psalm. In fact, this repeated expression sets into motion a cascading recital in verses 3-9 of the awesome power of the Lord in whose temple all can but cry, "Glory!" (v 9) to this Lord who is "enthroned" (twice repeated in v 10 in a chiastic arrangement with Yahweh as subject;

---

[87]Emphasis is Driver's. See *An Introduction to the Literature of the Old Testament*, 363.

יהוה : ישב :: וישב : יהוה), who gives strength and who blesses his people (יהוה יברך את-עמו; יהוה עז לעמו יתן, v 11). Adding to this information our prior finding that the first two verses employ a three-fold synonymous repetition of the phrase "ascribe to the Lord," I would maintain that this entire psalm is a carefully crafted poem that employs synonymous parallelism in an emphatic or climactic way. The psalm is an impassioned summons to "ascribe to the Lord" the glory that is due this Lord whose "voice" is so powerful. For it is this Lord who is "enthroned" over all who gives strength and blessings to "his people."

Of course, to analyze how repetitions function to organize a given literary unit is to move beyond Lowth's descriptive categories of parallelism. "Types" of parallelism—be they the three types described by Lowth, the five types described by Koch, or the six types described by Briggs—equip the critic with language to describe a figure of parallelism within a composition. But no matter how many types of parallelism are defined, a figure is still only a brief sub-unit within the larger literary structure. These figures often constitute the base for a discussion of a larger literary structure, but their isolation is only a first step in discerning the larger structure or architectural pattern of a composition.

From Lowth, I have acquired the basic tools necessary for isolating parallel elements in a given composition. The recognition of the variety in the number of corresponding elements and the diversity of the arrangements of these elements opens up new avenues in the discovery of correspondences in expanded literary units. His hints at the meaning of "constructive" or "synthetic" parallelism are of particular importance in the study of narrative. Lowth spoke of poetry and aimed at providing tools for translation. I will speak of narrative and will aim at providing tools for the discernment of architectural patterns in narrative compositions. While I will not adopt the use of the terms synonymous, antithetic, and constructive parallelism to describe narrative correspondences in my study, I remain indebted to Lowth for the ideas that generated the critical language I will employ in describing symmetries in the narrative structure of the Book of Judith.

The Influence of James Muilenburg

The scholar who has most clearly articulated the significance of repetitions in biblical compositions is James Muilenburg. Convinced that "the appearance of synonymity is seldom fortuitous or capricious,"[88] Muilenburg uncovered instances in which repetition conditioned the verbal

---

[88]Muilenburg, "A Study in Hebrew Rhetoric: Repetition and Style," VTSup 1 (1953) 97-111.

structure of an entire poem or composition.[89] He sketched the procedures of this kind of investigation in his 1968 Presidential Address to the Society of Biblical Literature. He described his orientation to the texts as follows:

> What I am interested in, above all, is in understanding the nature of Hebrew literary composition, in exhibiting the structural patterns that are employed for the fashioning of a literary unit, whether in poetry or in prose, and in discerning the many various devices by which the predications are formulated and ordered into a unified whole. Such an enterprise I should describe as rhetoric and the methodology as rhetorical criticism.[90]

Muilenburg delineated two major tasks for the rhetorical critic:

> (1) . . . to define the limits or scope of the literary unit, to recognize precisely where and how it ends.
> (2) . . . to recognize the structure of a composition and to discern the configuration of its component parts, to delineate the warp and woof out of which the literary fabric is woven, and to note the various rhetorical devices that are employed for marking on the one hand, the sequence and movement of the pericope, and on the other, the shifts or breaks in the development of the writer's thought.[91]

The key to discerning both the limits of the literary unit and the structure of its composition, or the macro-structure and the micro-structure of a text as it has been called,[92] is the recognition of repetitions.

As marks of the scope of the unit, Muilenburg mentions two important clues. First, the strategic appearance of repeated climactic lines. Second, the presence of an *inclusio* or ring composition "where the opening words are repeated or paraphrased at the close."[93] As marks of the warp and woof of the composition, Muilenburg discusses five literary devices: chiasmus, anaphora or repeated beginnings, refrains or repeated endings, repeated keywords, and strategic collocations of particles.[94]

---

[89]For examples, see ibid., 100ff.

[90]James Muilenburg, "Form Criticism and Beyond," *JBL* 88 (March 1969) 8.

[91]Ibid., 8-10.

[92]See Martin Kessler, "A Methodological Setting for Rhetorical Criticism," *Semitics* 4 (1974) 25.

[93]Muilenburg, "Form Criticism and Beyond," 9.

[94]Ibid., 11-17. In addition to these five literary devices, Muilenburg includes analyses of poetic clusters which he designates "strophes" (cf. pp. 11-13). Strophic definition is not germane to narrative analysis, hence it

Muilenburg was keenly concerned with the literary or rhetorical structure of Hebrew poetry and prose. But he was also expressly interested in biblical theology[95] and form criticism. It can be somewhat misleading to see his delineation of tasks for the rhetorical critic presented in summary form as above, because such a list bespeaks an exclusively text-centered orientation.[96] In his own works Muilenburg included text centered concerns, but they were employed alongside the more traditional approaches.[97] The title of his important study legitimating rhetorical criticism, "Form Criticism and Beyond," testifies to the inclusiveness of his critical concerns. Muilenburg said explicitly that rhetorical criticism was a supplement, not an alternative, to form criticism:

> Finally, it has not been our intent to offer an alternative or a substitute for it, but rather to call attention to an approach of eminent lineage which may supplement our form-critical studies. For after all has been said and done about the forms

---

has not been included here. It should be understood that Muilenburg nowhere *lists* these five literary devices, but rather that he employs them in the course of his discussion of the second task of the rhetorical critic, the discernment of the configuration of the component parts of a composition. The five literary devices listed here represent a summary of his discussion.

[95]Theological comments run throughout all of Muilenburg's works; see in particular, "Is There a Biblical Theology?" *USQR* 12 (1957) 29-37, where Muilenburg discusses the necessity of appreciating the characteristics of the Semitic way of thinking as a prerequisite to an adequate biblical theology. Cf. also his major study, "Introduction and Exegesis to Isaiah, Chapters 40-66," *IB* (ed. George A. Buttrick; New York: Abingdon, 1956) 5.381-773.

[96]Contemporary advocates of rhetorical criticism have produced studies which are entirely text-centered. In *Rhetorical Criticism: Essays in Honor of James Muilenburg,* see for example, Martin Kessler, "Rhetorical Criticism of Genesis 7," 1-17; Isaac M. Kikawada, "The Shape of Genesis 11:1-9," 18-32; or George Rideout, "The Rape of Tamar: A Rhetorical Analysis of 2 Sam 13:1-22," 75-84. In these studies, "form" is synonymous with "study of compositional structure." Interestingly, Muilenburg himself attends primarily to the study of the composition of Exod 15:1-18 in his "A Liturgy on the Triumphs of Yahweh," *Studia Biblica et Semitica: Theodoro Christiano Vriezen Dedicata* (ed. W. C. van Unnik and A. S. van der Woude; Wageningen: H. Veenman en Zonen, 1966) 233-51.

[97]For an assessment of Muilenburg's work, see Bernhard W. Anderson's introductory essay, "The New Frontier of Rhetorical Criticism: A Tribute to James Muilenburg," in *Rhetorical Criticism,* ix-xviii.

and types of biblical speech, there still remains the task of discerning the actuality of the particular text, and it is with this, we aver, that we must reckon, as best we can, for it is this concreteness which marks the material with which we are dealing. In a word, then, we affirm the necessity of form criticism, but we also lay claim to the legitimacy of what we have called rhetorical criticism. Form criticism and beyond.[98]

Muilenburg's fidelity to form criticism and the more traditional branches of biblical criticism no doubt grows out of the scholarly temper of his times. Muilenburg stood squarely among the best biblical critics of his day, and his scholarly publications[99] are presented in the traditional critical language of his period. He himself expressed special indebtedness to Hermann Gunkel, the "pioneer and spiritual progenitor"[100] of form criticism. Muilenburg's words about Gunkel show both his high regard for this scholar and his own sensitivity of the value of hermeneutics:

It is not too much to say that Gunkel has never been excelled in his ability to portray the spirit which animated the biblical writers, and he did not hesitate to draw upon the events of contemporary history or the experiences of the common man to explicate the interior meaning of a pericope.[101]

It is no exaggeration to say that Muilenburg in all his writings was able to animate the biblical stories and to explicate their theological meanings with a talent equal to that of Gunkel.[102] Like Gunkel, Muilenburg is remembered as a "pioneer and spiritual progenitor." But in spite of his professed allegiance to form criticism Muilenburg's name is associated with

---

[98]Muilenburg, "Form Criticism and Beyond," 18.

[99]For a listing of his works published prior to 1962, see R. Lansing Hicks, "A Bibliography of James Muilenburg's Writings," *Israel's Prophetic Heritage: Essays in Honor of James Muilenburg* (ed. Bernhard W. Anderson and Walter Harrelson; New York: Harper & Brothers, 1962) 233-42. For a listing of his works published after 1962, see Ivan J. Ball, Jr., "Additions to a Bibliography of James Muilenburg's Writings," *Rhetorical Criticism: Essays in Honor of James Muilenburg* (ed. Jared J. Jackson and Martin Kessler; Pittsburgh: Pickwick, 1974) 285-87.

[100]Muilenburg, "Form Criticism and Beyond," 1.

[101]Ibid., 2.

[102]In "A New Frontier of Rhetorical Criticism," Anderson says, "When it comes to grasping the interior, theological dimensions of Israel's faith, James Muilenburg is unexcelled, as those who have experienced his demanding and sensitive scholarship and the charismatic power of his teaching know" (p. x).

a kind of criticism that has enabled critics to move beyond form critical concerns.

In fact, in most recent applications of rhetorical criticism biblical scholars have taken as their primary point of orientation the text-centered concerns Muilenburg outlined in his famous Presidential Address.[103]   In calling this approach "rhetorical criticism," these biblical critics endorse the direction proposed by Muilenburg in a way that may be more exclusively text centered than he intended, even as they set aside concern about the definition(s) of rhetorical criticism as it is understood in contemporary literary study.[104]

If Muilenburg were still working today it would be interesting to know what he would say about wholly text-centered criticism and what he would add to the debate among English literary critics about the meaning of the words "rhetorical criticism." It was one of Muilenburg's special gifts that he was trained as both an English literary critic and as a biblical scholar.[105]

Traditionally, the study of the theory of rhetoric has been associated with Aristotle and with the effective use of language and argument as a means of persuasion. In the discourse of contemporary criticism, though, rhetoric is variously associated with a host of issues including questions of style, method, genre, theory, practice, and imagination versus will. In the face of all this imprecision and transition, Robert L. Scott and Bernard L. Brock point out that "the products of rhetoric . . . are multitudinous. Part of

---

[103]For example, see Lundbom, *Jeremiah*, 2. In addition, see the essays listed above in n. 96.

[104]In "A Methodological Setting for Rhetorical Criticism," Kessler claims that, "the basic problem with rhetorical criticism is that English literary critics are by no means agreed as to what that well-worn term 'rhetoric' signifies or ought to signify" (p. 22). For an English literary critic's view of this issue, see Murray Krieger, "Contextualism and the Relegation of Rhetoric," *The Play and Place of Criticism* (Baltimore: Johns Hopkins, 1967) 165-76. For an essay that witnesses to the fact that English literary critics are coming to terms with the confusion over the definition of rhetoric, see Marie Hochmuth Nichols, "Rhetoric and Style," *Patterns of Literary Style* (ed. Joseph Strelka; University Park: Pennsylvania State University, 1971) 130-43.

[105]For the details of Muilenburg's teaching career which began as an instructor in English composition at the University of Nebraska (1920-1923) and continued through his appointments in theology at Pacific School of Religion (1936-1945), Union Theological Seminary (1945-1963), and finally San Anselmo Theological Seminary (1963-1969), see Anderson, "The New Frontier of Rhetorical Criticism," x-xiii.

the task of rhetorical criticism is to find a focus, to pick products that will be fruitful to criticize."[106]

At present, English literary critics are themselves divided on the question of what is the most fruitful focus of rhetorical criticism. Three perspectives can be observed: (1) that of the traditional, neo-Aristotelian critics who are guided by Aristotle's principles as the basis of their work; (2) that of the experiential, eclectic critics who are guided by personal insights as the basis of their own work; and (3) that of the critics who accept the emerging "new rhetoric*s*," yet reject experiential centering as a basis of criticism as they look toward a unified theory of rhetoric that will equal that of Aristotelianism but that will be based in a system wholly outside that of Aristotle.[107]

In the wake of Edwin Black's frontal attack on Aristotle's principles in his 1965 publication *Rhetorical Criticism: A Study in Method*,[108] the critics have settled into a certain skeptical easiness with the impossibility of philosophical certainties about rhetoric. Radical scrutiny has produced not the death of rhetorical criticism but rather a kind of rebirth that is founded on the acceptance of paradox. Marie Hochmuth Nichols begins an essay entitled "Rhetoric and Style" with the following telling anecdote:

> Under a plane-tree, by the banks of the Ilissus, Socrates put a question to his friend Phaedrus, with whom he had been discussing rhetoric. "Do you know," said Socrates, "how you can speak or act about rhetoric in a manner which will be acceptable to God?" "No, indeed," said Phaedrus, and twenty-five hundred years later many of us would answer the question in the same way. We might also go on to say, as Socrates did, "If we had the truth ourselves, do you think we should care much about the opinions of men?"[109]

---

[106]Robert L. Scott and Bernard L. Brock, *Methods of Rhetorical Criticism: A Twentieth-Century Perspective* (New York: Harper & Row, 1972) 7.

[107]So Scott and Brock, *Methods of Rhetorical Criticism*, see esp. pp. 19-23, 123-27, 261-65. Following each of these sections of discussion of the traditional perspective, the experiential perspective, and the perspective of "new rhetorics" respectively, there appears a set of essays by noted proponents of each of these critical perspectives. The book is an unusually helpful primer of the varieties of rhetorical criticism.

[108]Edwin B. Black, *Rhetorical Criticism: A Study in Method* (New York: Macmillan, 1965).

[109]Nichols, "Rhetoric and Style," 130.

Knowing that it is impossible to know in an ultimate sense what rhetorical criticism really is, the critics nonetheless attend seriously to the pursuit of this knowledge.

Various assumptions and points of view differentiate the perspectives of rhetorical critics. Scott and Brock have outlined the major characteristics of the traditional, experiential, and "new rhetorics" perspectives in a helpful summary. They stress that these generalizations are possible only at the expense of omitted details, but they hope to aid self-conscious methodological reflection in their abstraction.[110] The following is Scott and Brock's summary of the three perspectives on rhetorical criticism:

The Traditional Perspective
1. *Orientation.* The critic concentrates on the speaker (or the apparent source of discourse). His purpose is to consider the speaker's response to the rhetorical problems that the speaking situation poses.
2. *Assumptions*
    a. Society is stable; people, circumstances, and rhetorical principles are fundamentally the same throughout history.
    b. Rhetoricians have discovered the essential principles of public discourse.
    c. Rhetorical concepts are reasonably discrete and can be studied apart from one another in the process of analyzing rhetorical discourse.
    d. A reasonably close word-thought-thing relationship exists. Rhetorical concepts accurately describe an assumed reality.
3. *Consensus.* Rhetoricians generally agree on what the ideal rhetorical process is.

The Experiential Perspective
1. *Orientation.* No single element or rhetorical principle can be assumed as the starting point for criticism. Thus, the critic, depending on his sensitivity and knowledge, must make the fundamental choice of emphasis.
2. *Assumptions.*
    a. Society is in a continual state of process.
    b. An infinite combination of concepts, strategies, and principles are available for the study of public discourse.
    c. Any system of categorizing is arbitrary and does not accurately reflect an assumed external reality for extended periods of time.

---

[110]Scott and Brock, *Methods of Rhetorical Criticism,* 339.

3. *Consensus.* No special pattern exists for the study of public discourse. Therefore, discourse must continually be studied afresh.

The Perspective of the "New Rhetorics"

1. *Orientation.* Rhetoric and criticism must find a starting point in the interaction of man and his social environment.

2. *Assumptions.*
    a. Society is in process, but fairly stable relationships can be found that govern man's interactions with his environment.
    b. A flexible framework may be constructed for the study of public discourse.
    c. Man's symbol system influences his perceptions of reality.

3. *Consensus.* A unified rhetorical framework is necessary for the productive study of rhetoric and criticism.[111]

Scott and Brock conclude that in writing rhetorical criticism, a critic will benefit from consciously delineating (1) the focus of a given study; (2) the critical vocabulary that is the best instrument for a particular study; and (3) the perspective or starting point of the critical inquiry; (4) the sort of judgment—descriptive, interpretive, or evaluative—that the critic wishes to make; and finally, (5) the end to which a particular study is directed.[112]

In the case of Muilenburg and his understanding of rhetorical criticism, we can see that these concerns were indeed inherent in his critical act. Muilenburg did not express the concerns in a programmatic fashion, but by examining his article, "A Liturgy on the Triumphs of Yahweh,"[113] which he said "represents an attempt to subject a passage to rhetorical analysis,"[114] we can see how he expressed these concerns in the context of this particular study. The focus of his study is expressed as an interest in understanding "the composition of the passage in its present form."[115] This focus is the unifying point of reference in a study in which Muilenburg seeks "to examine the ways in which the writer's Semitic ways of thinking are articulated into Semitic ways of speech."[116] Muilenburg's concentration is on the text itself, and his orientation to rhetorical criticism sems grounded in what literary critics call "the traditional perspective."[117] While being

---

[111]Ibid., 339-40.

[112]Ibid., 340-41.

[113]For full bibliographical reference, see above, n. 96.

[114]Muilenburg, "A Liturgy on the Triumphs of Yahweh," 250.

[115]Ibid., 251; cf. the discussion on pp. 245ff.

[116]Ibid., 250.

[117]See Scott and Brock, *Methods of Rhetorical Criticism*, 21-100.

traditional in perspective from a rhetorical critical point of view, Muilenburg's focus is on questions that he acknowledged were outside the established biblical approaches of "historical or literary criticism, of *Gattungkritik,* or of traditio-historical criticism."[118]

His critical vocabulary in "A Liturgy of the Triumphs of Yahweh" includes words like poetic composition, motif, framework, strategic rhetorical collocation or climactic contexts, hymn, liturgy or litany, form and structure, rhetorical features, hymnic refrains, strophes, key words, parallelism, figures or images, colon, bicolon, repetition, stylistic and structural difficulties, and meter. As an instrument, this critical vocabulary was one that was readily understood by other biblical critics. Muilenburg expanded the function of an established critical language to describe the relationship of the parts of a particular text as a compositional whole.

The critical perspective or starting point for this rhetorical study is an acceptance of the text in its received form. Repeatedly throughout his article he stresses that "it is best to take the liturgy as we have it here before us at the present time to attempt to follow the course of its thought and the sequence of the bicola as they advance to their goal."[119] He credits the Semitic writer with a compositional plan, and Muilenburg's goal is to uncover this compositional pattern.

Muilenburg's conviction that a text has a meaningful and coherent compositional structure colors the sorts of judgments he makes. When it comes to "what may appear to us to be irregularities and infelicities"[120] in a text, he works with these difficulties and does not alter the text to resolve these problems.[121]

In the area of judgment, Muilenburg puts forward findings that are variously descriptive, interpretive, and evaluative. He describes the composition of the given text that its message may be made manifest to us; he interprets the influence this message may have had on its Semitic audience; and he evaluates the theological importance of this composition for us. At this point in his criticism, Muilenburg does something unique, if Scott and Brock are correct in their evaluation of the three perspectives in current rhetorical critical practice when they make the claim that:

> Traditional criticism tends to be primarily descriptive, and the
> criticism typifying the new rhetorics tends to be primarily

---

[118]Muilenburg, "A Liturgy on the Triumphs of Yahweh," 251.
[119]Ibid., 245.
[120]Ibid., 246.
[121]Ibid.; cf. the discussion on pp. 246ff.

interpretive. In general, rhetorical critics have backed away from the evaluative. Too often, however, we believe that critics have failed to think through the implications of their choice of purpose.[122]

Muilenburg says explicitly that his work is not merely "an aesthetic exercise."[123] He regards rhetorical criticism as "an exegetical tool."[124] The theological nature of the texts he analyzes causes the kinds of judgments he makes in his rhetorical analysis to differ from those made by English literary critics.

So, too, the end that he wishes to achieve by his analysis differs from the end sought by English literary critics. Muilenburg seeks understanding of the composition of texts not merely for the purpose of building up a rhetorical theory of biblical composition, but rather for the broader exegetical goal of theological appreciation.[125] The following lengthy quotation from "Form Criticism and Beyond" shows how closely intertwined study of composition and interpretation of meaning were for Muilenburg:

> It is often said that the Hebrew writers were not motivated by distinctively literary considerations, that aesthetics lay beyond the domain of their interests, and that a preoccupation with what has come to be described as stylistics only turns the exegete along bypaths unrelated to his central task. It may well be true that aesthetic concerns were never primary with them and that the conception of *belles lettres*, current in ancient Hellas, was alien to the men of Israel. But surely this must not be taken to mean that the OT does not offer us literature of a very high quality. For the more deeply one penetrates the formulations as they have been transmitted to us, the more sensitive he is to the rôles which words and motifs play in a composition; the more he concentrates on the ways in which thought has been woven into linguistic patterns, the better able he is to think the thoughts of the biblical writer after him. And this leads me to formulate a canon which should be obvious to all: a responsible and proper articulation of the words in their linguistic patterns and in their precise formulations will reveal to us the texture and fabric of the writer's thought, not only what it is that he thinks, but as he thinks it.[126]

---

[122]Scott and Brock, *Methods of Rhetorical Criticism,* 341.
[123]Muilenburg, "A Liturgy on the Triumphs of Yahweh," 250.
[124]Ibid.
[125]Ibid.
[126]Muilenburg, "Form Criticism and Beyond," 7.

The "Rules of My Game"

The assumption that form and content are inseparable underpins my own approach to rhetorical criticism. My work is grounded on the principle that to understand literary structure is to comprehend meaning. In doing rhetorical criticism, or what I would prefer to call compositional analysis, my focus is identical to that expressed by Muilenburg in that my intent is to describe the composition of the Book of Judith in its present form. The text itself is the primary generator of the critical data of this study.

The critical language of my study depends most heavily on a vocabulary rooted in the concepts of parallelism that Lowth defined. In the next chapter when I discuss expressed identities, expressed antitheses, implied antitheses, and artificial identities, I will be using a vocabulary that has evolved out of a union of Lowth's description of correspondences between parallel or repeated terms and of Muilenburg's description of the architectural unity of compositions. Diagrams and tabular summaries illustrating compositional correspondences also play a significant part in the critical vocabulary of my study. In addition, the more traditional descriptive literary vocabulary articulated by Muilenburg and others[127] will be employed.

The perspective or starting point of my critical inquiry is the scriptural text itself. With Muilenburg, I credit the author with a compositional plan. Our job is to discover how the theology of this narrative has been clothed in its particular compositional structure, or, to borrow a metaphor, how the wine and the water have been mixed. The author of 2 Maccabees says of his own composition, a work abbreviating the longer history of Jason of Cyrene:

> If it is well told and to the point, that is what I myself desired;
> if it is poorly done and mediocre, that was the best I could do.
> For just as it is harmful to drink wine alone, or again, to drink
> water alone, while wine mixed with water is sweet and delicious
> and enhances one's enjoyment, so also the style of the story
> delights the ears of those who read the work.
>
> 2 Macc 15:38-39

---

[127]See, e.g., above pp. 42. Cf. also Rideout's discussion of literary/rhetorical terminology in "Prose Compositional Techniques in the Succession Narrative," passim. Richard A. Lanham, *A Handlist of Rhetorical Terms: A Guide for Students of English Literature* (Berkeley: University of California, 1969), is a helpful compendium of classical rhetorical terms.

The judgments that I will put forward in this study are in the main descriptive.   My primary interest is in discerning the compositional architecture of the text.   Though I firmly believe that to articulate this architectural pattern properly is to confront the meaning of the composition, I am convinced that "description" of this compositional structure and "interpretation" of it are two distinct critical tasks.   This distinction becomes clearer when we consider the analogy of how music critics approach the study of musical compositions.   If in a conservatory, a class in compositional analysis were assigned a particular Beethoven sonata, the entire class would be expected to produce identical or nearly identical descriptions of the structure or form of this sonata.   There is only one correct description of the formal compositional elements of the piece. However, if in a conservatory this same group of students were in a class in performing piano and were now assigned to perform this same sonata, each playing of it would be individual.   To perform the sonata demands individual interpretation, and interpretations will vary as the talents and skills of the various interpreters vary.   Thus, describing an artist's work is different from performing it.   Description is primarily an objective, commonly verifiable task, though it most assuredly is tempered by the subjective skill of the critic.   Interpretation, on the other hand, is primarily a subjective, individually validated, critical task, though it is tempered by the objective measure of the composition being performed.[128]

Earlier in this chapter when I stated that the particular type of rhetorical criticism that I will do might best be called compositional analysis, I did so for the very reason that I believe that valid rhetorical criticism can legitimately present either objective or subjective judgments, or even both.   In the name of rhetorical criticism as Muilenburg proposed it, texts can be analyzed for descriptive compositional data or they can be "performed" in the sense that objective descriptive data can serve as the basis for theological interpretation or evaluation of a more subjective kind.[129]   The methodological orientation of my work is to that aspect of rhetorical criticism that should be able to be submitted to external verification.   Others who analyze the composition of the text of Judith

---

[128]For another interpretation of this issue, see Fishbane, *Text and Texture,* 8f.   Cf. his comments on p. xiii.

[129]I consider the kind of rhetorical criticism that Phyllis Trible presents in *God and the Rhetoric of Sexuality* (Philadelphia: Fortress, 1978) an example of a literary/rhetorical "performance" of the highest quality in which the descriptive compositional data are both interpreted and evaluated in a reading informed, among other things, by feminist hermeneutics.

should be able independently to reproduce my findings if they are valid, though the language we use to describe our findings might at this time vary since we are still in the process of formulating the critical language of this kind of study.

The end to which my description of the composition of the Book of Judith is directed is exegetical. Since this is confessional literature, my study assumes a theological purpose for the narrative. As we come to a better understanding of the composition of the Book of Judith, I submit that the theological meaning of this work will be more clearly perceived.

To recapitulate, then, and to bow to the wisdom of Tucker's insistence that the critical enterprise requires a shared set of game rules, let me say that I will follow the procedures that Muilenburg outlined for the rhetorical critic.[130] To describe the "warp and woof," or texture of the compositional units in the Book of Judith, I will rely on a kind of language that has developed out of Lowth's categories of parallel members. In Chapter III, I will describe the external architectural structure which organizes the story as a whole. In Chapter IV, I will describe the internal composition of the narrative units delineated in Chapter III. In Chapter V, I will speculate on the relationship of the compositional data that this study has generated to the larger issues of (1) worship in Israel, (2) the position of women in the patriarchal world, (3) the sectarian alignment of the Book of Judith, and finally (4) the effectiveness of rhetorical critical study as a tool for analyzing imaginative theological literature.

───────────────

[130]Cf. the discussion above, p. 35. These concerns are, as we noted earlier, wholly text-centered. They do not incorporate form critical interests except in the broadest sense that form criticism and rhetorical criticism are interested in defining the limits of the unit under consideration. This study cannot in any serious way be considered a form critical study of the Book of Judith. However, as Roy F. Meleugin says, "His [Muilenburg's] method serves better than genre analysis as the starting point in exegesis, particularly for texts which exhibit artistic formulations" ("Muilenburg, Form Criticism, and Theological Exegesis," *Encounter With the Text* [ed. Martin J. Buss; Philadelphia: Fortress, 1979] 93). It may be that literary/rhetorical criticism serves ultimately as the best beginning point for a form critical study. But the work of the form critic will not be pursued here.

III

External Design
of the Book of Judith

The Book of Judith is a self-defined literary unit of sixteen chapters. It opens with an introduction to the powerful King of the Assyrians, Nebuchadnezzar (1:1), and it closes with a note about the long lasting influence of a woman of Israel, Judith (16:25). The narrative is structured in two parts, each with its own dominant character: Nebuchadnezzar, the King of Assyria, governs the actions of Part I (chapters 1-7); Judith, a widow of Bethulia, leads the way in Part II (chapters 8-16).[1]

The story itself is a contest over who is the true God, the true lord and master of the world, Nebuchadnezzar or Yahweh. Holofernes stakes the claim that his king, Nebuchadnezzar, is the sovereign God; Judith risks her life and reputation backing the belief that her God, Yahweh, is the true God. Much like 1 Kings 18, which records the contest between Elijah and the prophets of Baal on Mt. Carmel, the Book of Judith tells a story in which the enemy of Israel takes the lead in the contest.[2] Part I narrates the military

---

[1]Notable exceptions to the two-part division of the text are represented in the following studies. P. Winter, "Book of Judith," *IDB* (ed. George Arthur Buttrick; New York: Abingdon, 1962) 1024, divides the story into three parts: chapters 1-3, Nebuchadnezzar against the non-Jewish nations; chapters 4-7, the general situation in Judea and the particular situation in Bethulia; and chapters 8-16, the story of Judith. Ernest Haag, *Studien zum Buche Judith: Seine theologische Bedeutung und literarische Eigenart* (Trier: Paulinus, 1963), discusses the text in three chapters titled as follows: Die Bedrohung Israels durch die gottfeindliche Macht des Nabuchodonosor (Kap. 1-3); Das Gottesvolk in der Bedrängnis (Kap. 4-8); and Die Errettung des Gottesvolkes (Kap. 9-16). Haag's inclusion of chapter 8, the introduction of Judith and her summoning of the town officials as separate from chapters 9-16 is most unusual.

[2]In both 1 Kings 18:20-40 and the Book of Judith, one character stands against the many: Elijah stands against the four hundred fifty prophets of

aggressions of the Assyrian enemy and Israel's near submission to their rule. Part II records Judith's reaction to the compromising tendencies of her community and her actions in effecting the defeat of the Assyrian threat. In the end, Yahweh triumphs through the courage and daring of this woman. On her account, her people survive and "no one ever again spread terror among the people of Israel in the days of Judith, or for a long time after her death" (16:25).

A PRÉCIS OF THE STORY

Part I of the story begins as Nebuchadnezzar attacks Arphaxad in his seemingly impenetrable capital city, Ecbatana. Narration records Nebuchadnezzar's request for auxiliary troops from his vassal nations, and their disregard of his request. Despite the fact that the vassal nations do not come to his aid, Nebuchadnezzar triumphs greatly over Arphaxad (1:1-15).

Nebuchadnezzar and his troops return home to Nineveh for a grand celebration of the victory. After a time, Nebuchadnezzar commissions Holofernes, his commander-in-chief, to lead a punitive expedition against the rebel nations. As these troops sweep across the nations of the west, fear and terror overwhelm those who have not been punished for their resistance and some send envoys to sue for peace. Despite their surrender, Holofernes demolishes their cultic sites and destroys their gods, "so that all nations should worship Nebuchadnezzar only, and all their tongues and tribes should call upon him as god" (3:8).

Hearing of these desecrations, greatly terrified, and fearful for the safety of their own Temple, the people of Israel prepare to defend Jerusalem. The High Priest Joakim leads in the making of battle strategies and the whole of Israel cries to God for help (4:1-15).

Angered at the continued insubordination of this one nation, Holofernes summons the Canaanite leaders of his assemblage and demands an explanation of this foolish resistance (5:1-4). Achior, the leader of the Ammonites, dares to tell him that the Israelites have an ancient and well-established history of special protection by a God who does not abandon them as long as they do not sin. Achior counsels that Holofernes avoid

---

Baal and the mute community of Israel (1 Kings 18:21-22); Judith stands against the hoard of Nebuchadnezzar and the cowardice of her community, saying in her prayer that she knows that Yahweh's "power does not depend upon numbers" (Judith 9-11). Both stories contain delightful mocking scenes (cf. 1 Kings 18:27-29 and Jdt 10:11-13:10a). And in both stories, the objective of the faithful character is to have all know that Yahweh is God (cf. esp. 1 Kings 18:37-39 and Jdt 9:14).

military confrontation with these people, for such an attack may involve entanglement with their powerful God. But Holofernes scorns his advice:

> And who are you, Achior, and you hirelings of Ephraim, to prophesy among us as you have done today and tell us not to make war against the people of Israel because their God will defend them? Who is God except Nebuchadnezzar? (6:2)

Then Holofernes orders that his slaves bind and deliver Achior to Bethulia, the Israelite town which is the locus of the Assyrian attack, so that Achior will share the fate of the people of Israel.

When Achior has been abandoned at the foot of the hill below Bethulia, the men of the town rescue him and bring him before their magistrates: Uzziah, Chabris, and Charmis. Before an assembly of the entire town, Achior recounts all that has taken place in the council of Holofernes. Further shaken by these details, the people of Bethulia cry out to their God for help. Achior is consoled and praised, and he and the elders go to the house of Uzziah for a banquet. "And all that night they called on the God of Israel for help" (6:21).

The next day, Holofernes and all his cohorts move against the little town. Great terror seizes the people of Bethulia when they see the vast enemy armies encamping in the valley below their town. They fear that Bethulia, though well-protected by the mountains, will not be able to sustain the burden of so great an enemy. On the second day, in full view of the Bethulians, Holofernes studies the approaches to the town and at the foot of the mountain examines the springs which supply its water. His advisors suggest that he destroy the town by cutting off its water supply and thus avoid the loss of so much as one soldier. They point out that an assured victory will cost the Assyrians nothing but time (7:9-15).

As the first part of the book comes to a close, thirty-four days have passed and the people of Bethulia are overwhelmed by thirst and panic. They gather around Uzziah and their other town officials to demand that the town be surrendered:

> For it would be better for us to be captured by them; for we will be slaves, but our lives will be spared . . . (7:27).

Uzziah urges them to take courage but agrees that if relief does not come within five days he will do as they wish. He postpones their surrender, but his words do nothing to relieve his people. The inadequacy of this compromise is poignantly told in the closing words of Part I, "And they were greatly depressed in the city" (7:32c).

Part I ends on this bleak note. The people have declared that all is lost:

> For now we have no one to help us; God has sold us into their hands . . . (7:25).

Short of a miracle, it seems that soon the people of Bethulia will be worshiping Nebuchadnezzar.

Part II, chapters 8-16, opens as Judith, a widow living in Bethulia, hears of Uzziah's plan to surrender in five days. Greatly troubled, she summons him and the magistrates of the town to her house where she upbraids their lack of faith. Her long speech (8:11-27) shows a profound understanding of the effects which compromise and surrender will have for Israel. She unequivocally declares that what they have done is wrong: "Who are you, that have put God to the test this day?" (8:12). She defends the freedom of God, saying:

> Do not try to bind the purposes of the Lord our God, for God is not like man to be threatened, nor like a human being, to be won over by pleading.

> Therefore, while we wait for his deliverance, let us call upon him to help us, for he will hear our voice, if it pleases him (8:16-17).

Judith reminds the leaders that capture will mean the destruction of the sanctuary in Jerusalem, that slavery is apostasy. She exhorts them to set an example for the people: "In spite of everything let us give thanks to the Lord our God, who is putting us to the test as he did our forefathers" (8:25). Her words are spoken out of the conviction that true faith has no limits. She flatly says that God alone has the right to test and set conditions.

When she finishes speaking, Uzziah replies to her in words that betray his continued defense of his actions and his steadfast hope for a miracle:

> All you have said has been spoken out of a true heart, and there is no one who can deny your words. Today is not the first time your wisdom has been shown, but from the beginning of your life all the people have recognized your understanding, for your heart's disposition is right. *But* the people were very thirsty, and they compelled us to do for them what we have promised, and made us take an oath which we cannot break. *So pray for us*, since you are a devout woman, and the Lord will send us rain to fill our cisterns and we will no longer faint (8:28-31, emphasis added).

Ignoring Uzziah's self-justification and flattery,[3] Judith declares that she has a plan (8:32). While she gives no hint of precisely what she plans, she does claim that the Lord will deliver Israel by her hand before the five days of the postponement prior to the surrender have passed. The magistrates sanction her venture, agree to meet her later that evening at the town gate, and leave (8:35-36).

Once alone, Judith prays that God grant her success (9:1-14). Then she prepares herself by removing her everyday garments of sackcloth and putting on her most festive clothing (10:1-4). Next she gathers together a bag of ritually pure food and utensils (10:5). Then she and her maid go out to the town gate where the magistrates await her arrival. The leaders of the town are greatly impressed by her lovely transformation and pray that God will bless her. Judith once again pauses to worship God, then asks the men to order that the gate be opened for herself and her maid (10:9). She still has not told any of the details of her scheme to anyone and we can only wonder how the magistrates feel as they watch the two solitary women go out from the city that evening. Totally unarmed they depart at a time of day when Judith's great beauty makes her vulnerable to assault.

Indeed, before the women have gone far, they are met by an Assyrian patrol (10:11). The soldiers are greatly struck by Judith's beauty and humorously stumble over one another choosing a group of one hundred from their number to accompany her to the tent of Holofernes (10:17). Once together, Judith and Holofernes have a lengthy conversation (11:1-12:4) in which truth and hypocrisy are subtly intertwined. Both tell outright lies in their attempt to impress the other. Holofernes, forgetting his mistreatment of Achior, urges Judith to take courage saying, "I have never hurt anyone who chose to serve Nebuchadnezzar" (11:1). Judith counters with the false promise that she is there to help him by telling him when Israel has sinned, "and then you shall go out with your whole army, and not one of them will withstand you" (11:18). Following this meeting, Judith spends three uneventful days in the enemy camp. Each passing day makes more likely the surrender of Bethulia, but finally on the fourth day Holofernes plans a party to which he has his servant invite Judith (12:13).

---

[3]According to Dancy, Uzziah's response is "that of a weak man, chiefly concerned to justify himself. He cannot go back on his word (no *oath* was actually mentioned in 7:31), so he asks Judith to help him meet it by praying for what at that time of year would be a miracle (1 Sam 12:17)." See *The Shorter Books of the Apocrypha*, 100.

Judith and Holofernes meet a second time at this banquet. They both eat and drink a good deal (12:17-20), and the party seems a great success. Evening comes and all the other guests depart from Holofernes' tent leaving Judith and Holofernes alone together (13:1). The time of conquest has arrived, but on account of all that he has drunk, Holofernes has fallen asleep on his bed (13:2). Thus the unexpected advantage of the moment belongs to Judith. As before all her other major actions in the narrative, she first pauses to pray. Then she takes Holofernes' own sword and chops off his head. She gives the severed head to her maid who is waiting outside the tent as instructed. The maid puts the head into the food bag, and the two women once again go out unaccompanied into the darkness of the night (13:10).

Her return to Bethulia excites and encourages her people. They forget their great thirst in the fervor of the moment. All assemble to hear her tale of triumph; then they join with Uzziah in blessing her accomplishment. She instructs her people to hang Holofernes' head on the parapet of the city wall and urges them to go out against the Assyrians when morning comes (14:1-4). But before they hang the head on the wall, she asks that Achior be brought to look on it. Achior confirms that the head is indeed that of Holofernes and seeing what the "God of Israel" has done, "he firmly believed in God, and was circumcised, and joined the house of Israel, remaining so to this day" (14:10). Then the people put the head of Holofernes on the wall of their town and go forth to annihilate their enemies.

When the Assyrians see the Bethulians coming, they send word to rouse Holofernes who they suppose is sleeping with Judith. Instead, they discover that he is dead (14:15). Panic overcomes them and they try to flee. The Bethulians together with the other Israelites rush upon them and slaughter them (15:5-7). Joakim, the High Priest of Jerusalem, arrives to see all that has taken place. And he and his officials bless Judith as "the exaltation of Jerusalem," the "great glory of Israel," and the "pride of the nation" (15:9).

The Israelites plunder the enemy camp for thirty days (15:11). Then the women join with Judith in leading a triumphant procession to Jerusalem where all the people worship Yahweh who has delivered Israel by the hand of the woman Judith (15:12-16:20). The book closes with a description of how Judith lived out the rest of her life as a faithful widow in the house of her husband Manasseh until her death at the age of one hundred and five. Her fame grew and on her account, no one threatened Israel for a long time after her death (16:25).

SYMMETRIES BETWEEN PART I AND PART II

Repetition is the major organizational feature of this narrative. Formal symmetries occur between the two halves of the story as well as within each of the two parts of the book. These inventive repetitions function to define the limits of each half of the story and to fix the relationship of these two parts as that of one whole, the Book of Judith. First, we shall examine the corresponding features that bind Part I and Part II of the story. These correspondences are of four types: (1) expressed identities, (2) expressed antitheses, (3) implied antitheses, and (4) artificial identities.

Expressed identities are correspondences between the halves of the story in which two parallel passages of similar meaning share at least one set of equivalent or identical terms.

(1) The first act of the leading character is to send for others: Nebuchadnezzar "sent" (ἀπέστειλεν) to all who lived in Persia (1:7); Judith "sent" (ἀποστείλασα) her maid to summon the magistrates (8:10).

(2) At a gathering of their own calling, both leading characters claim to have a plan: Nebuchadnezzar "called together" (συνεκάλεσεν) his officers and nobels and set forth a "secret plan" (τὸ μυστήριον τῆς βουλῆς) which he recounts fully (2:2); Judith "called" (ἐκάλεσεν) Chabris and Charmis, the elders of her city (8:10) and told them that she had a plan (πρᾶξιν), the details of which she refused to discuss (8:34).

(3) Both claim to execute the plan through their own hand (ἐν χειρί μου): Nebuchadnezzar says, "What I have spoken *my hand* will execute" (2:12); Judith, "The Lord will deliver Israel by *my hand*" (8:33).

(4) "Feasts" (πότον) are held to honor guests: Uzziah entertains Achior (6:21); Holofernes entertains Judith (12:10).

(5) Actions judged arrogant are indignantly challenged: Holofernes says to Achior, "Who are you" (καὶ τίς εἶ σύ) to utter such foolish words (6:2); Judith says to the magistrates, "Who are you" (καὶ νῦν τίνες ἐστὲ ὑμεῖς) to set yourselves up in the place of God (8:12).

(6) Worship is explicitly urged: Holofernes demands that all tribes call upon Nebuchadnezzar as God (ἐπικαλέσωνται αὐτὸν εἰς θεόν, 3:8); Judith urges the leaders of her town to join her in calling upon Yahweh (ἐπικαλεσώμεθα αὐτὸν, 8:17).

(7) The conclusions of each half of the story describe the enemy in distress: the Israelites are "greatly disturbed" (ἐταράχθησαν σφόδρα, 7:4) at the end of Part I; the Assyrians are in "great dismay" (ἐταράχθη . . . σφόδρα, 14:19) at the end of Part II.

Expressed antitheses are correspondences between the halves of the story in which two parallel passages in direct opposition to each other share at least one set of equivalent or identical terms.

(1) Holofernes and Judith execute opposing plans: Holofernes carries out "the plan" (τῆς βουλῆς, 2:2) of Nebuchadnezzar; Judith chastises the officials of her town for daring to interfere with "the plan" (τὰς βουλὰς, 8:16) of Yahweh.

(2) For one set of reasons, "fear and trembling of him [Holofernes] fell" (ἐπέπεσεν φόβος καὶ τρόμος, 2:28) upon the rebel nations; for quite another set of reasons "trembling and fear fell" (ἐπέπεσεν . . . τρόμος καὶ φόβος, 15:2) upon the Assyrian troops when they heard of the death of their leader.

(3) Face to face encounters with Holofernes occasion radical alterations in Achior's group membership. After the first meeting in which he tells the story of Israel's special relationship with Yahweh, Achior is expelled from the Assyrian camp. Holofernes says to him, "You shall not see my face (τὸ πρόσωπόν μου) again from this day until I take revenge on this race that came out of Egypt. . . . And if by chance thou dost hope in thy heart that they will not be taken, let not thy face fall (μὴ συμπεσέτω σου τὸ πρόσωπον)" (6:5, 9). After the second meeting, in Bethulia "when he [Achior] came and saw the head (τὴν κεφαλὴν) of Holofernes in the hand of one of the men at the gathering of the people, he fell on his face (ἔπεσεν ἐπὶ πρόσωπον) and became as one dead" (14:6). On this account, Achior "joined the house of Israel" (14:10).

(4) Pledges of honesty to Holofernes are both true and false. Achior says, "I will tell you the truth about this people" (5:5), and he does. Judith says, "I will tell nothing false to my lord this night" (11:5) but she lies.

In addition to these expressed antitheses, there are implied antithetical correspondences between the halves of the story in which implicitly parallel elements of the story are sharply contrasted with each other.

(1) The executors of the respective plans are sexual opposites: Holofernes is male: Judith is female.

(2) The executors of the respective plans employ strikingly dissimilar weapons: Holofernes uses military might to fight his battle; Judith uses beauty and wisdom to win her triumph.

(3) Conditional and unconditional faith are contrasted. The coercive religious practices (prayers, sackcloth, and ashes) of the Israelites

who stipulate conditions for their continued belief in the power of Yahweh (cf. especially 7:24ff.) are opposed by the truly pious practices (prayers, sackcloth, and ashes) of Judith who openly chastises any attempt to bind the purposes of Yahweh (cf. especially 8:10ff.).

(4) The central opposition of the book is the contention over the identity of the true God. The question which subtly motivates the entire narrative is who is most powerful: Nebuchadnezzar or Yahweh. Part I details a powerful military conquest; Part II tells of a courageous woman's belief that her God will not abandon her or her people. The details of this contest are the very fabric of the book. In chapter 16, Judith sings a song of praise to Yahweh "who crushes wars" (16:3) and foils the enemy "by the hand of a woman" (16:6). Her God is the triumphant "Lord Almighty" (16:6).

Artificial identities further reinforce the narrative unity of Part I and Part II of the Book of Judith. These are subtle grammatical or functional correspondences between parallel passages in the respective halves of the story. There is no explicit synonymy or antonymy of terms between passages of this sort; the correspondences are artificially implied by sets of skillfully matched components.

(1) A prose introduction to the leading character opens each part of the narrative: 1:1-6 describes Nebuchadnezzar; 8:1-8 describes Judith. These two passages contain the following artificially parallel components:

(a) Both open with a temporal phrase: "In the twelfth year of the reign of Nebuchadnezzar" (1:1); "At that time Judith heard about these things" (8:1).

(b) Both identify the leading character: Nebuchadnezzar is the King of the Assyrians; Judith is the daughter of Merari and the widow of Manasseh.

(c) Both describe the present activity of the leading character: Nebuchadnezzar is busy capturing the Medes; Judith is involved in living the life of a pious widow.

(2) Once the respective plans for punishment and deliverance have been set in motion, the one carrying out the plan makes food preparations: Holofernes is the doer of the preparations for his army (2:18); Judith is the doer of the preparations for herself and her maid (10:5). The identity between these two passages is artificial: Holofernes is the grammatical subject of the food preparation episode in Part I; Judith is the grammatical subject of the parallel episode in Part II. In all other details, the two passages differ.

(3) A specified and an implied three-day period precedes the enactment of the respective plans: Holofernes marches "three days" (τριῶν ἡμερῶν, 2:21) before he begins his purge of the nations; Judith spends three uneventful days in the Assyrian camp, where "on the fourth day" (ἐν τῇ ἡμέρᾳ τῇ τετάρτῃ, 12:10) Holofernes invites her to the fateful banquet.

(4) Similarly, a specified and an implied thirty-four day period is significant to the enactment of the respective plans: the Assyrians surround Bethulia for "thirty-four days" (ἡμέρας τριάκοντα τέσσαρας, 7:20);[4] Judith spends a total of four days in the Assyrian camp (cf. 12:10) after which the Israelites plunder the enemy for "thirty days" (ἡμέρας τριάκοντα, 15:11).

(5) The narrative procedures for implementing the respective plans are similar in that each depends on a set of capture terms. "Fear and terror" spreads (2:28; 4:2; 7:4) as a direct result of Holofernes' "ravaging, plundering, destroying, sacking, and burning" the cities through which he passes (see 2:23-27 for the initial statement of this pool of terms). Self-seductive "marvelling" spreads (10:7, 14, 19, 23) as a direct result of Judith's "great beauty and wisdom" (see 8:7-8 for the initial statement that Judith is very beautiful and feared God, i.e., was wise. Her wisdom is confirmed by Uzziah in 8:29; her great beauty in 10:7. Both are universally acknowledged by every male she meets through Part II of the story). The effects of the two plans are artificially parallel in that those who come into contact with Holofernes in Part I and then with Judith in Part II are undone, both physically and emotionally, by a given set of terms which are carefully defined at the introduction of the respective character's work in the narrative.

These many shared correspondences illustrate formal literary proportion and balance between the two halves of the Book of Judith. The compositional counter-balances in the text itself directly challenge Cowley's description of the book's two divisions: (1) the introduction (chapters 1-7) and (2) and story of Judith (chapters 8-16);[5] and they call into serious question his assessment of these two parts:

> The book is thus almost equally divided between the introduction and the story proper. The former is no doubt somewhat out of

---

[4]For variant readings of the length of the siege, see Enslin and Zeitlin, *Judith,* 106, n. 20.

[5]Cowley, "Judith," 242.

proportion, and the author dwells at rather unnecessary length on the military details. In spite, however, of these defects of composition, the literary excellence of the work is universally recognized even through the uncomely disguise of the Greek translation.[6]

Cowley's work on Judith appears in R. H. Charles' classic collection, *The Apocrypha and Pseudepigrapha of the Old Testament*. First published in 1913, this work continues to exert considerable influence on those who study the intertestamental literature. Thus it is of particular importance to refute Cowley's description of Part I as "out of proportion" with Part II and to declare untrue his statement that Part I is marred by "defects of composition."

These two judgments—that Part I is out of proportion with and compositionally inferior to Part II—are perpetuated in the recent critical studies of Alonso-Schökel and Dancy. In speaking of the heroine, Judith, Alonso-Schökel says the following:

The main character enters the stage late, almost too late. In terms of extension, almost in the middle (Chapter 8); in terms of events, when almost everything is lost. More than one exegete, evaluating this fact, finds in the story a lack of proportion, namely that the extension of the first part (1-7) is not justified by the narrative function it fulfills.[7]

In speaking of the literary merits of the Book of Judith, Dancy, a scholar whom Alonso-Schökel calls "the most perceptive reader,"[8] makes the following comments:

The first part (chapters 1-7) is duller in thought and flatter in style. Its aim is to give a historical setting for a historical deed, but it does so without the economy or the accuracy that a modern reader looks for.[9]

The first part of the book is so much weaker that one would like to reserve the title 'author' for the writer of chapters 8 to the end. But apart from anything else, the crucial character of Achior spans the two parts, so one must judge the book as a whole.

---

[6]Ibid., 242-43.
[7]Alonso-Schökel, "Narrative Structures," 3.
[8]Ibid.
[9]Dancy, *The Shorter Books of the Apocrypha*, 67.

The historical setting has few merits. Dramatically it is
spoiled by tedious descriptions (especially 1:2-4, 4:9-15) and
confusions (e.g. 2:21-7), stylistically by exaggerations (e.g. 1:16)
and empty rhetoric (e.g. 2:5-13).[10]

Two recently published surveys of the non-canonical Jewish literature
also echo prejudice against Part I. Leonhart Rost simply ignores Part I. In
his first sentence describing the contents of the Book of Judith, he says,
"The narrative focuses on an heroic act on the part of Judith to deliver
Bethulia, a city besieged by Holofernes, one of Nebuchadnezzar's generals."[11] Nichols de Lange also dismisses Part I. He tells the story of chapters 1-7 in one paragraph, and the story of chapters 8-16 in over thirteen
pages.[12] The negative bias towards chapters 1-7 continues and is reinforced
by recent studies.

Elsewhere I have suggested that, "Any study which puts aside chapters
1-7 too quickly renders itself—not the narrative—out of proportion."[13] Here
I should like to restate that assertion and to add that it is in Part I of the
book that the audience finds its place in the narrative. Not many who listen
to the Book of Judith identify fully with the evil embodied by Nebuchadnezzar or Holofernes or with the goodness portrayed by Judith. The
audience is, I suspect, more like the wavering Israelites who are blind to
their own resources. The cry, "We have no one to help us" (7:25), voices a
timeless and universal human experience of abandonment.

In his book, *The Uses of Enchantment*, Bruno Bettelheim makes a
strong case for the human enrichment allowed by participation in stories
that permit us to externalize our own difficulties by looking at the wishes
and anxieties of others. Bettelheim does not speak of the Book of Judith,
but his words are germane to our discussion. He says that a good story
communicates the message:

> . . . that a struggle against severe difficulties in life is unavoid-
> able, is an intrinsic part of human existence—but that if one
> does not shy away, but steadfastly meets unexpected and often
> unjust hardships, one masters all obstacles and at the end
> emerges victorious.[14]

---

[10]Ibid., 68.

[11]Leonhard Rost, *Judaism Outside the Hebrew Canon: An Introduction
to the Documents* (trans. David E. Green; Nashville: Abingdon, 1976) 53.

[12]De Lange, *Apocrypha*, 114-28.

[13]Toni Craven, "Artistry and Faith in the Book of Judith," *Semeia* 8
(1977) 79.

[14]Bruno Bettelheim, *The Uses of Enchantment: The Meaning and
Importance of Fairy Tales* (New York: Vintage, 1977) 8.

From a psychological perspective, Judith is the good story that it is precisely because of chapters 1-7. Here the audience participates in Israel's struggle to survive; in Part I the audience watches Israel attempt to cope with unjust hardships. It is here that the listeners see Israel's plan of action and its error, namely its binding of the purposes of God to suit a desire for guaranteed survival. Faced with disaster, the people of Bethulia plead with their leaders to make peace with the Assyrians. The Israelites decide that God has failed them; indeed they say, "God has sold us into their hands" (7:25b). And so they call upon their leaders to make a compromise with the enemy, "For it would be better for us to be captured by them; for we will be slaves, but our lives will be spared, and we shall not witness the death of our babes before our eyes, or see our wives and children draw their last breath" (7:27). Without chapters 1-7, the impact of the story would be greatly weakened. Part I gives a depth and proportion to the meaning of the story that should not be minimized because of scholarly disappointment with the geographical and historical details of chapters 1-7.[15]

As a whole, the Book of Judith sets out a two-part contest over the sovereignty of opposing super powers: Part I argues the case for Nebuchadnezzar's supremacy; Part II argues the case for Yahweh's supremacy. The kind of literary balance evidenced in the many correspondences between the halves of the book suggests the hand of a highly skilled writer who meant the subject of this story to be told in two parts. It is important to understand that Part I, with a tag ending describing the surrender of Bethulia, would be a tragic but complete story. Similarly, Part II, with a brief introduction explaining the reasons for Judith's summoning of the officials of Bethulia, would be a triumphant, equally complete story. But alone neither Part I nor Part II tells the same story that is told in the Book of Judith.

The inner organization of each half of the Book of Judith further evidences the balance and interdependence of the two parts of the story. Finely crafted repetitions order each of the halves of the story, additionally confirming both the literary importance of each of the halves of the book and the literary integrity of the book as a whole.

---

[15]Cowley concludes that the author "had a not very exact knowledge" of history ("Judith," 243). Brockington finds it a "disappointment" that the book contains no reliable historical information (*Apocrypha*, 44). Eissfeldt suggests that the story shows "how little the author knew history" (*Introduction*, 586).

THE ARCHITECTURAL COMPONENTS OF PART I

As can be seen from the following sketch of Part I, there is no cause to say with Dancy that "the first part of the book is so much weaker that one would like to reserve the title 'author' for the writer of chapters 8 to the end."[16] The literary units in Part I unfold in a chronological sequence[17] that shifts from geographic setting to setting with both cohesion and balance. The literary units are in a logical cause/effect relationship. Assyrian aggression is countered by Israelite reaction. The following scheme displays the orderliness of Judith 1-7:

1. Introduction to Nebuchadnezzar and his campaign against Arphaxad (1:1-16)
2. Nebuchadnezzar commissions Holofernes to take vengeance on the disobedient vassal nations (2:1-13)
3. Development

   A   The campaign against the disobedient nations; the people surrender (2:14-3:10)

   B   Israel hears and is "greatly terrified"; Joakim orders war preparations (4:1-15)

   C   Holofernes talks with Achior; Achior is expelled from the Assyrian camp (5:1-6:11)

   C'   Achior is received into Bethulia; he talks with the people of Israel (6:12-21)

   B'   Holofernes orders war preparations; Israel sees and is "greatly terrified"[18] (7:1-5)

   A'   The campaign against Bethulia; the people want to surrender (7:6-32).

---

[16]Dancy, *The Shorter Books of the Apocrypha*, p. 68.

[17]Cf. Alonso-Schökel's comment, "The development of the first part (1-7) is clear and, except for the speech of Achior, strictly chronological" ("Narrative Structures," 4). The exception of Achior's speech is somewhat confusing, because Achior appears logically in the story after Holofernes has requested an explanation from his troops (cf. Jdt 5-6). Strictly speaking, the only break in chronological order occurs in Jdt 7:17 where the Assyrians seize the water supply to Bethulia which it seemed they had already seized in Jdt 7:7.

[18]The phrases translated identically in B and B' as "greatly terrified" differ in Greek: ἐφοβήθησαν σφόδρα σφόδρα (4:2) and ἐταράχθη- σαν σφόδρα (7:4). The RSV translators rightly pick up the parallel nature of these verses. On the expansive vocabulary of the author of Judith, see Enslin and Zeitlin, *Judith*, 115, n. 15.

The preceding diagram shows that once the narrative has been set into motion, a threefold chiastic pattern orders the execution of Nebuchadnezzar's revenge on the nations: (1) A and A' are war stories that culminate in the desire to surrender; (2) B and B' are war preparations and references to Israel's great terror; and (3) C and C' are movements from the camp of Holofernes to the town of Bethulia occasioned by conversations with Achior.

Achior's movement from the Assyrian camp (Section C) to the Israelite town (Section C') provides a pivot or turning point in the narrative structure of Part I. These two sections, the structural heart of the first half of the story, line up the opponent parties in the book: Assyria and the God Nebuchadnezzar are counterpoised against Israel and the God Yahweh. Section C, Achior's recital of Israel's sacred history, prompts the Assyrians to voice the central question of Part I, indeed of the entire book, "Who is God except Nebuchadnezzar?" (6:2). Manipulative acts of literal and penitential violence surround Achior's claims to Holofernes about the unassailable protection afforded Israel by the covenant with Yahweh and his report to the Bethulians of the effects he suffered as a result of making these claims. The Assyrians put their faith in their military might; the Israelites put their faith in conditions of their own making: they pray loudly with a great show of ritual mourning, but give Yahweh five days to deliver them. By the end of Part I, Achior appears to be a condemned fool, Nebuchadnezzar seems to be the God triumphant, and the Bethulians dejectedly await the day of their surrender to Assyria.

Each literary unit in the chiastic pattern ordering the development section of Part I (2:14-7:32) is defined by a major geographic shift of scene and an alternation between the nations of Assyria and Israel. Each of the literary units in the chiastic pattern opens with a temporal clause introduced by either a pleonastic καί, in simple juxtaposition with a second verb in the pattern of the Hebrew waw-conversive, or by the particle δέ followed by a temporal phrase (2:14; 4:1; 5:1; 6:12; 7:1; 7:6). A, B', and A' each contain a sub-section in which a second nation becomes the subject of the literary unit (2:28; 7:4; 7:19). These sub-sections are each separated from the preceding portions of the narrative by the same temporal pattern that marks the major literary units; the sub-sections are also introduced by a pleonastic καί or by the particle δέ followed by a temporal phrase. In sum, these geographic, national, and temporal alternations have a domino effect in the narrative movement of Part I. As a row of dominoes set on end topples once the first one is knocked down, so the nations successively capitulate to Assyria. The supremacy of Assyria is confirmed as "terror" sweeps across first the empire at large (2:28), then Judea (4:2), and finally Bethulia (7:4). The following is a summary of the formal elements that define the literary units of the chiastic pattern in Part I:

A   Scene: Assyrian armies in Nineveh move against the nations; the nations react in fear and terror

"καὶ Holofernes left the presence of his master . . ." (2:14).

"καὶ fear and terror of him fell upon all the people who lived along the seacoast . . ." (2:28).

B   Scene: Israelites in Judea

"καὶ the people of Israel living in Judea heard of everything that Holofernes, the general of Nebuchadnezzar the king of the Assyrians, had done to the nations . . ." (4:1).

C   Scene: Assyrians' camp outside Judea

"καὶ Holofernes, the general of the Assyrian army, heard that the people of Israel had prepared for war . . ." (5:1).

C'   Scene: Israelites in Bethulia

"καὶ ὡς (when) the men of the city which was on the crest of the mountain saw them, they took up their weapons . . ." (6:12).

B'   Scene: Assyrians' camp outside Bethulia; Israel reacts in terror

"τῇ δὲ ἐπαύριον (the next day) Holofernes ordered his whole army, and all the allies who had joined him, to break camp and move against Bethulia . . ." (7:1).

" οἱ δὲ (but) the people of Israel, ὡς (when) they saw their great host, were greatly disturbed . . ." (7:4).

A'   Scene: Assyrian armies move against Bethulia; the people of Bethulia react in terror

"τῇ δὲ ἡμέρᾳ τῇ δευτέρᾳ (on the second day) Holofernes led out all his cavalry in full view of the Israelites in Bethulia . . ." (7:6).

"καὶ the people of Israel cried out to the Lord their God, for their courage failed . . ." (7:19).

THE ARCHITECTURAL COMPONENTS OF PART II

Part II of Judith is as equally well-designed as Part I. The distribution of leading roles in Part II, however, is strikingly different from that in Part I. Unlike Part I with its alternation of subjects in successive literary units, Part II is entirely dominated by Judith. She is the leading character in every literary unit in the second half of the narrative. Once Judith takes the stage in chapter 8, she shares it with others but surrenders it to no one. The following scheme displays the orderliness of Judith 8-16:

A   Introduction to Judith (8:1-18)

B   Judith plans to save Israel (8:9-10:9a)

C   Judith and her maid leave Bethulia (10:9b-10)

D   Judith overcomes Holofernes (10:11-13:10a)

> > └ └ L C' Judith and her maid return to Bethulia (13:10b-11)
> >   └   B' Judith plans the destruction of Israel's enemy (13:12-16:20)
> > └   A' Conclusion about Judith (16:21-25)

As in Part I, so also in Part II a threefold chiastic pattern (A-B-C-C'-B'-A') orders the narrative. Once again a pivotal movement from the camp of the Assyrians to the town of Bethulia (C-C') signals the center of the composition. However, in Part II, this pivotal movement frames a distinct and important sequence: Judith's time in the Assyrian camp and the murder of Holofernes. Section D, as the heart of the chiastic pattern which structures Part II, breaks the symmetry of the threefold chiastic architecture shared by the two halves of the book and resolves the question posed at the center of the pattern in Part I (C-C'): "Who is God except Nebuchadnezzar?" (6:2). Both the form and content of Section D signal the climactic significance of Judith's triumph over Holofernes and the "god" he represents.

Each literary unit in the chiastic pattern of Part II is introduced by a temporal clause indicated either by a pleonastic καί in simple juxtaposition with a second verb in the pattern of the Hebrew waw-conversive or by the particle δέ followed by a temporal phrase.[19] Judith's movements dominate and define the narrative sequences of Part II. The following is a summary of the formal elements that define these units:

A   A narrative introduction to Judith, a widow of Bethulia
  "καί ἤκουσεν ἐν ἐκείναις ταῖς ἡμέραις (and in those days) Judith heard about these things: she was the daughter of Merari, the son of Ox, son of Joseph, son of . . ." (8:1).

B   Scene: Judith at home in Bethulia
  "καί Judith heard the wicked words spoken by the people against the ruler, because they were faint . . ." (8:9).

C   Scene: Judith and her maid leave Bethulia
  "καί ἐξῆλθοσαν (then they went out) to the city gate of Bethulia and found Uzziah standing there with the elders of the city . . ." (10:6).

D   Scene: Judith in the Assyrian camp
  "καί the women went straight on through the valley; and an Assyrian patrol met her . . ." (10:11).

C' Scene: Judith and her maid return to Bethulia
  "καί ἐξῆλθον (then) the two of them (went out) together, as they were accustomed to go for prayer; and they passed through the camp . . ." (13:10b).

---

[19]On the use of δέ, see Enslin and Zeitlin, *Judith*, 121, n. 1.

B'   Scene: Judith in Bethulia
        "καὶ the men of her city heard her voice, they hurried down to
        the gate of the city . . ." (13:12).
A'   A narrative conclusion about Judith, a widow of Bethulia
        "μετὰ δὲ τὰς ἡμέρας ταύτας (after these days) everyone
        returned home to his own inheritance, and Judith went to
        Bethulia . . ." (16:21).

The corresponding units in this chiastic structure share parallel introductory patterns. A and A' open with specific indications of time: ἐν
ἐκείναις ταῖς ἡμέραις (8:1); τὰς ἡμέρας ταύτας (16:21). B and
B' begin with καὶ plus the verb "to hear": καὶ ἤκουσεν (8:9); καὶ
ἐγενέτο ὡς ἤκουσαν (13:12). C and C' with καὶ plus the verb "to go
out": καὶ ἐξῆλθοσαν (10:6); καὶ ἐξῆλθον (13:10b). There is a tran-
quil simplicity in the design and balance of Part II which reinforces the quiet
dominance of Judith. On a certain "day" (8:1) she appears in the story; she
"hears" (8:9) of the travesties being considered by her community; and she
"goes out" (10:6) from her town to effect the deliverance of her people; she
destroys the enemy (Section D, 10:11-13:10a); then she "goes out" (13:10b)
from the enemy camp to return to her home in Bethulia; the men of her town
"hear" her voice (13:12) and obey her command to annihilate the enemy
troops; after these "days" (16:21) when her people have been secured she
withdraws from public view and returns to her private way of pious
observance until her death at one hundred five years old.

        In sum, the external design of the Book of Judith is a beautifully
executed two-part structure, each part of which is ordered by a threefold
chiastic pattern. Two introductory sections precede the chiastic pattern of
Part I which is distinguished by its national and geographic alterations. An
extra sequence, Section D, framed by a chiastic pattern, distinguishes the
structure of Part II. While no one character dominates all of the sequences
in Part I, Part II focuses entirely on Judith as the representative of
Yahweh. Her appearance cancels the tumult caused by Holofernes, the representative of Nebuchadnezzar, in Part I. Yahweh triumphs by the hand of
the woman, Judith. Formal symmetries between the halves of the story, as
well as within each of the two parts, define the elegant balance which marks
the design of the narrative and the resolution of its conflict over the identity
of the true God. The whole of the Book of Judith and both its halves stand
as finely crafted examples of narrative art.

IV

Internal Structural Patterns
in the Book of Judith

Having defined the external architectural design of the Book of Judith as a whole composed of two halves each of which is chiastically contoured, we shall turn now to an examination of the parts of this whole. We shall investigate certain features of the internal compositional patterns which both undergird the unity of the narrative and reinforce its meaning.[1] We shall observe the identical, contrary, and formal grammatical patterns of repetition[2] of specific words, phrases, and ideas which order the internal structure of the narrative.[3] Thus working with the narrative components defined in the previous chapter, here we shall examine more closely selected features of the inner construction of the individual units.[4]

PART I, SECTION ONE (1:1-16) AND
SECTION TWO (2:1-13)

Part I opens with two compact literary sections whose form and content stand apart from the chiastic structure which orders the first half of the narrative. Section One (1:1-16) and Section Two (2:1-13)[5] introduce Nebuchadnezzar first as a military aggressor against the Medes and then as a

---

[1]Martin Kessler suggests the terms macro-structure and micro-structure to describe the distinction between the study of the whole of a piece of literature and the study of its parts. See "A Methodological Setting for Rhetorical Criticism," 25.

[2]Cf. Chap. III, 53ff.

[3]For a helpful summary of the rhetorical terms used to describe repetitive patterns, see Richard A. Lanham, *Rhetorical Terms* (Berkeley: University of California, 1969) 124-25.

[4]See the summaries of Part I: Judith 1-7 and of Part II: Judith 8-16 in Chap. III, 60, 62-63 respectively.

[5]Ibid., 60.

military despot ordering an attack against his own vassal nations that dared
to refuse him assistance in the battle against the Medes. The two sections
function as a preface explaining the background to the subsequent confrontation between Assyria and the nations. Nebuchadnezzar makes his only
appearance in the story in these two sections, and he delivers his only
speech, his words of instruction to Holofernes (2:5-13) here. Together Section One and Section Two handily establish Nebuchadnezzar as a mighty
authority in his dealings both abroad and at home. He refers to himself as
"the Great King, the lord of all the earth" (2:5), and his boast is well sup-
ported in these opening sections of the narrative.

Section One (introduction to Nebuchadnezzar and his campaign
against Arphaxad, 1:1-16) and Section Two (Nebuchadnezzar commissions
Holofernes to take vengeance on the disobedient vassal nations, 2:1-13) both
begin with grammatically similar[6] pseudo-historical phrases designating a
specific time for the ensuing actions ("In the twelfth year" of his reign
Nebuchadnezzar attacks Arphaxad, 1:1; "In the eighteenth year" of his reign
Nebuchadnezzar orders a revenge against his vassals, 2:1). Both opening
passages designate Nebuchadnezzar as the historically impossible king of the
Assyrians[7] with Nineveh as his specified (1:1) and implied ("in the palace,"
2:1) geographic setting. These correspondences are highlighted in the
following segments of the opening passages of Section One and Section Two:

Ἔτους δωδεκάτου τῆς βασιλείας Ναβουχοδονοσορ,
ὃς ἐβασίλευσεν ᾿Ασσυρίων ἐν Νινευη τῇ πόλει τῇ
μεγάλῃ . . . (1:1).

Καὶ ἐν τῷ ἔτει τῷ ὀκτωκαιδεκάτῳ δευτέρᾳ καὶ
εἰκάδι τοῦ πρώτου μηνὸς ἐγένετο λόγος ἐν οἴκῳ
Ναβουχοδονοσορ βασιλέως ᾿Ασσυρίων . . . (2:1).

Section One continues with a description of the military contest between two extraordinarily powerful kings: Arphaxad and Nebuchadnezzar.
Arphaxad, the king of the Medes, is attacked in his strongly fortified capital
city, Ecbatana. The narrative does not record the details of the military

------

[6]Synthetic parallelism in Lowth's terminology. See Chap. II, 26-28.

[7]Nebuchadnezzar, of course, was a Babylonian king (605-562 B.C.E.).
His father, Nabopolassar, together with Cyarxes the king of the Medes,
destroyed Nineveh and its Assyrian king Sin-shar-ishkun in 612 B.C.E. For
further discussion, see in particular Siegfried Herrmann, *A History of Israel
in Old Testament Times* (Philadelphia: Fortress, 1975) 263-65, and John
Bright, *A History of Israel* (Philadelphia: Westminster, 1972) 314-15.

confrontation between these two super powers,[8] but rather focuses on a tallying of those vassal nations who do and those who do not support Nebuchadnezzar in his attack. Many nations joined (συνήντησαν) Nebuchadnezzar (1:6). Others, however, designated as "inhabitants of all the earth" (πᾶσαν τὴν γῆν), refused "because they were not afraid of him (ἐφοβήθησαν) but looked upon him as only one man" (1:11). Although involvement with Arphaxad postpones more than sworn revenge upon the disobedient "inhabitants of all the earth" (πᾶσαν τὴν γῆν, 1:12), the stage has been set for a monumental retaliation against these peoples. Section One concludes with the notice that "in the seventeenth year" (1:13),[9] Nebuchadnezzar captures Arphaxad, his armies, and his city. Nebuchadnezzar and his troops then returned to Nineveh where they "rested and feasted for one hundred and twenty days" (1:16).

In Section Two, Nebuchadnezzar, the self-acclaimed "Great King, the lord of all the earth" (ὁ κύριος πάσης τῆς γῆς, 2:5), spells out the details of his "secret plan" (τὸ μυστήριον τῆς βουλῆς, 2:2) of revenge against the disobedient vassal nations. Holofernes is appointed to lead one hundred and twenty thousand foot soldiers and twelve thousand cavalry (2:5) in an attack on all the lands that disobeyed (εἰς συνάντησιν πάσῃ τῇ γῇ, 2:6). Thus in the eighteenth year of the reign of Nebuchadnezzar (2:1), the plan of retaliation is set into motion.

Nebuchadnezzar is angry with the vassal nations because, in his own words, "they have disobeyed the word of my mouth" (τοῦ στόματός μου, 2:6). The word "mouth" appears a total of three times in Section Two.[10] In

---

[8]The city of Ecbatana figures in the stories of Tobit and Judith. This city was the capital of the Medes and according to Ezra 6:2, the Edict of Restoration was preserved here. Little is known about this city, since no written documents in the Median language have been discovered, and since no thorough archaeological work has been undertaken here as the modern Iranian city of Hamadan is built on top of the ancient site of Ecbatana. Enslin cites two texts of Herodotus which describe Ecbatana as surrounded by seven sets of concentric walls (1, 98) and Babylon as having walls whose dimensions exceed even those of the huge walls of Ecbatana which are described in Jdt 1:2-4 (i, 178). See Enslin and Zeitlin, *Judith*, 59-60, nn. 1, 2. See also M. J. Dresden, "Ecbatana," *IDB*, 2.6-7, and "Media," *IDB*, 3.320.

[9]"Not impossibly a reflection of Jer. 32:1," so Enslin and Zeitlin, *Judith*, 64, n. 13.

[10]The word "mouth" (στόμα) appears a total of seven times in Judith: 2:2, 3, 6 27; twice in 5:5; and once in 15:13. The chiastic arrangement of terms in 5:5 is particularly attractive, "The mouth of your servant . . . will

two references prior to the instance just cited in Jdt 2:6, the text says that Nebuchadnezzar recounted his secret plan of revenge with his own "mouth" (2:2), and that his followers decreed that they would destroy those who did not obey the word of Nebuchadnezzar's "mouth" (2:3). Ironic humor marks these three occurrences of the word στόμα in Section Two (2:2, 3, 6). Nebuchadnezzar's followers professing grand devotion pledge the destruction of those who have disregarded the word of his "mouth"; but before the story ends they too will be guilty of doing something other than that which the mouth of Nebuchadnezzar instructs them to do (cf. 2:10-11). In the end, Nebuchadnezzar's declaration, "they have disobeyed the word of my mouth" (2:6) is true of everyone. Despite many flourishes of obedience or disobedience, no one pays much attention to the words of the mouth of this powerful leader. He himself makes public what "his own mouth" has declared is a secret plan of retaliation (2:2).

Nebuchadnezzar's own words to Holofernes include the following instructions:

> You shall go and seize all their territory for me in advance. They will yield themselves to you, and you shall hold them for me till the day of their punishment. But if they refuse, your eye shall not spare and you shall hand them over to slaughter and plunder throughout the whole region (2:10-11).

Nebuchadnezzar vows, "I have spoken and I will do this by my own hand" (λελάληκα καὶ ποιήσω ταῦτα ἐν χειρί μου, 2:12). This important assertion that it is "by my hand" reappears in Part II of the book when Judith too makes the claim that "by her hand" a plan will be effected to deliver Israel (ἐν χειρί μου, 8:33, 9:9, 12:4). Without getting ahead of the story, we must take special note here of Nebuchadnezzar's statement that "by his hand" revenge against the nations will be executed. He rounds out his commands to Holofernes with the caution:

> Take care not to transgress any of your lord's commands, but be sure to carry them out just as I have ordered you; and do not delay about it (2:13).

Assertions of lordship frame Nebuchadnezzar's words to Holofernes (2:5-13). The speech opens with the statement that Nebuchadnezzar is "the Great King, the lord (κύριος) of the whole earth" (2:5), and it closes with the caution "do not transgress any of your lord's (κυρίου) commands"

---

tell you the truth . . . no lie will come forth from the mouth of your servant."

(2:13). Nebuchadnezzar's complaints against the nations are political and he frames his plan of political revenge in appropriate language. His vassals have shunned his authority, his "lordship," and they must pay for their foolishness. For all his arrogance, nowhere does Nebuchadnezzar claim the title "god" (Θεός) for himself. Ironically, Holofernes transgresses his "lord's" commands when he forces the nations "to worship Nebuchadnezzar only" and "to call upon him as god" (Θεόν, 3:8).[11] Holofernes makes this adjustment in his orders himself, thus failing to heed Nebuchadnezzar's specific caution to do exactly as ordered (cf. 2:13).

Similar patterns of grammar and language in Sections One and Two add to the symmetry and balance of the opening sections which document the fearsome authority of Nebuchadnezzar. As we have already noted, both sections begin with specific historical designations of a particular year in the reign of Nebuchadnezzar (1:1; 2:1). Besides adding a "familiar biblical touch" by mentioning a "precise year, month, and day,"[12] these historical references are so coordinated as to make the retaliation against the disobedient nations begin in the catastrophic year 587 B.C.E.[13] Both sections employ the verb συναντάω in crucial passages about the nations. Though

---

[11]Nebuchadnezzar's name appears alone as a proper noun only in 1:12, 11:7, and 12:13. The name is accompanied by the explicative "king" in 1:5, 2:19, 3:2, 11:4, 11:23, and 14:18. The phrase "king of the Assyrians" modifies the name in 1:1, 1:7, 1:11, 2:1, 2:4, 4:1. Nebuchadnezzar is described as a "god" only in 3:8 and 6:2 by Holofernes who does later call Nebuchadnezzar the "lord of all the earth" in 6:4 and the "king of all the earth" in 11:1 and 11:7.

I disagree with Alonso-Schökel's assertion that, "in the book Nebuchadnezzar is a kind of god, issuing orders, acting through others, and demanding adoration" ("Narrative Structures," 13). Ernest Haag makes a similar assertion in his discussion of "die gottfeindliche Macht" of Nebuchadnezzar (Judith, 9ff). In the book, Nebuchadnezzar acts like a powerful king who defeats powerful enemies. His combat is with an earthly king, Arphaxad, and his complaint is with nations who refused him auxiliary troops. To say that he acted like a god is to claim more than the story permits.

[12]Enslin and Zeitlin, Judith, 65, n. 1.

[13]The historical Nebuchadnezzar came to the throne of Babylonia in the year 605 B.C.E. Thus the eighteenth year of his reign would be 587 B.C.E., the date when Jerusalem indeed did fall to Babylonia under the leadership of Nebuchadnezzar. Pfeiffer points out that the events described in the story all take place within a few months, with the exception of the epilogue in 16:23-25 (New Testament Times, 293). Thus the entire story is imagined as having occurred in 587 B.C.E.

English translations do not show this correspondence, the Greek verbs are identical.[14]   In Section One, Nebuchadnezzar is "met" in the sense of "joined" (συνήντησαν) by many nations in his attack on Arphaxad (1:6). In Section Two, Nebuchadnezzar commissions Holofernes to "meet in battle" or "attack" (συνάντησιν) the disobedient nations (2:6).

In both Section One and Section Two, anger (ἐθυμώθη, 1:12; θυμῷ μου, 2:7) moves Nebuchadnezzar, the self-acclaimed lord of "all the earth" (πάσης τῆς γῆς, 2:5) to take vengeance on all the rebel nations. Eight times, the two sections make reference to Nebuchadnezzar's control over "all the earth" (πάσης τῆς γῆς):[15]

1:11   Nebuchadnezzar's vassals, "all who dwelt in all the land" (πάντες οἱ κατοικοῦντες πᾶσαν τὴν γῆν) made light of his call for auxiliary troops.

1:12   Nebuchadnezzar is greatly enraged at "all the land" (πᾶσαν τὴν γῆν) and swears vengeance against its inhabitants.

2:1   There is talk in the house of Nebuchadnezzar about the vengeance that is to fall on "all the land" (πᾶσαν τὴν γῆν).

2:2   Nebuchadnezzar tells his retainers and grandees about "all the wickedness of the land" (πᾶσαν τὴν κακίαν τῆς γῆς).[16]

2:6   Nebuchadnezzar commissions Holofernes to go against "all the land" (πάσῃ τῇ γῇ).

2:7   Nebuchadnezzar says that his wrath shall veil "all the face of the land" (πᾶν τὸ πρόσωπον τῆς γῆς).

2:9   Nebuchadnezzar pledges to lead the captives to the ends "of all the earth" (πάσης τῆς γῆς).

2:11   Nebuchadnezzar vows that those who disobey shall not be spared, but given over to slaughter and booty "in all thy land" (πάσῃ τῇ γῇ σου).[17]

---

[14]For these distinctions, see συναντάω in Henry George Liddell and Robert Scott, A Greek-English Lexicon, With a Supplement (Oxford: Clarendon, 1968) 1676.

[15]These references add to the imaginative character of Nebuchadnezzar's control. They seem best not taken literally; here as elsewhere in the story, the geographical details of the book are purely imaginary.

[16]The Greek context of this phrase is difficult. See Enslin and Zeitlin, Judith, 66, n. 2, for a summary of the alternate translations of this passage.

[17]Here, too, the Greek text is difficult. Commentators are troubled by the phrase, though it can be explained as it stands in the text. Some versions omit σου; others replace it with του. See Robert Hanhart, Judith, 59, n. 11, for a summary of the various text traditions. See also Enslin and Zeitlin, Judith, 68, n. 11.

The repetition of the phrase "all the earth" in Section One and Section Two emphasizes the wide scope of Nebuchadnezzar's authority. This "lord of all the earth" is not one to enrage for he who "utterly destroyed" Arphaxad (1:15) can surely do the same to any who challenge him. He who rested for "one hundred and twenty days" (ἡμέρας ἐκατὸν εἴκοσι, 1:16) has at his control "a hundred twenty thousand soldiers" (χιλιάδας ἐκατὸν εἴκοσι, 2:5). In effect, these two carefully crafted opening sections establish a set of credentials for Nebuchadnezzar that show it was utter folly for the nations "not to fear" (οὐκ ἐφοβήθησαν, 1:11) him.

In an imaginative way, Section One (1:1-16) and Section Two (2:1-13) set the story in the realm of fantasy. Illusions abound in the historical and geographical details of the opening sections. Contrary to what the story says, the historical Nebuchadnezzar did not rule the Assyrians; he was, in fact, a Babylonian king (605-562 B.C.E.), the dreaded Babylonian king who captured Jerusalem in the year 587 B.C.E. Nineveh was never Nebuchadnezzar's capital city; his own father, Nabopolassar, had had a hand in destroying this city in 612 B.C.E. Arphaxad was never a king of the Medes, nor did he ever build mighty protective walls around Ecbatana. According to Herodotus, Dioces fortified Ecbatana around 700 B.C.E.[18] Nebuchadnezzar did not capture Ecbatana; Cyrus, king of Persia, performed this deed in 550 B.C.E. Nebuchadnezzar never made war on Media,[19] nor is it known that he ever had a general who bore the Persian name Holofernes.[20]

In reality, Nebuchadnezzar was never "the lord of all the earth." The only true detail in the opening sections of the story is the association of Nebuchadnezzar's name with a massive military aggression occurring in the year 587 B.C.E. The eighteenth year of the reign of Nebuchadnezzar (cf. 2:1) was the year in which Jerusalem fell to Babylon. This was the year in which the historical Nebuchadnezzar did indeed move against Israel in an unforgettable confrontation. But while this date was historically traumatic,

---

[18]So Enslin and Zeitlin, Judith, 58, n. 1.

[19]Babylonia under Nabopolassar and Media under Cyaxares were allies in the campaigns (620-605 B.C.E.) that led to the final downfall of Assyria. Enmity did exist between Media and Assyria, however, and from the time of Sargon until about the middle of the seventh century, Media seems to have been subject to Assyria. See M. J. Dresden, "Media," IDB, 3.319-20.

[20]Citing Diodorus, Oesterly (Apocrypha, 177) points out that Holofernes (or Orophernes) was the brother of the Cappodocian king Ariarathes, the vassal of Artaxerxes Ochus (359-338 B.C.E.). This Holofernes fought successfully under the Persian king in one of his Egyptian campaigns (Diodorus xxxi.19, 2-3). Holofernes was also the name of a mid-second century B.C.E. Cappodocian king (Diodorus xxxi.32).

the other details in the opening sections of the book are historical and geographic fabrications. In speaking of the effect of the opening passages of
the book, Dentan says,

> This is like putting a modern story "in the days of Woodrow
> Wilson who was president of the Confederate States of America
> shortly after the end of World War II." Such confusion can
> hardly be other than deliberate and is perhaps intended to warn
> the reader against taking the story as literal history.[21]

Charles Cutler Torrey credits the author and the audience of that day
with a sympathetic understanding of the meaning of these conflated details:

> These events are imagined to have taken place after the return
> of the Jews from captivity, and after the rebuilding of the
> temple (4:3; 5:19). This is indefinite enough, and the narrator
> warns against any desire to make it more definite. He takes
> pains to tell his hearers plainly that they are listening to fiction,
> not to an account of the actual happenings. Those were the days
> when Nebuchadnezzar "reigned over the Assyrians in Nineveh,"
> and when Arphaxad "reigned over the Medes in Ecbatana" (1:1).
> Here he gives his auditors a solemn wink. It is just as though a
> modern story-teller should say: It happened at the time when
> Napoleon Bonaparte was king of England, and Otto von Bismarck
> was on the throne in Mexico. The Jewish novelist shows his
> humor, as well as his care for the right appreciation of his
> work. He knew that the readers and hearers of his own day, the
> young and the old alike, would see his meaning.[22]

Torrey has observed that, "the humor and its purpose are quite lost on
our modern commentators, who, without exception, believe the author of the
narrative to be aiming to give it a real historical setting, and are astonished
at his ignorance."[23] This was true in 1945, and unfortunately it is still true
in many modern assessments of Judith. Even Torrey himself fell into the
trap of literalizing an aspect of Judith by trying to establish a real geographical setting for the story. His conviction that Bethulia is a pseudonym
for Shechem is the portion of his work on Judith most often quoted in other
studies.[24]

---

[21]Dentan, *Apocrypha*, 56.

[22]Charles Cutler Torrey, *The Apocryphal Literature* (New Haven: Yale
University, 1945) 89-90.

[23]Ibid., 89, n. 82.

[24]Torrey made the claim that, "in one important property of the Judith
story, the geography and topography of the principal scenes, its author is

The Book of Judith simply does not yield literal or even allegorical data. Instead, its opening details seem to be a playful manipulation of both historical and geographical facts and inventions. The author's proclivity to imaginative fabrication continues throughout the entire story, even to the making up of a town so important in the story, Bethulia.[25] The historical and geographical absurdities point not to ineptitude on the part of the author,[26] but rather to skillfulness in focusing attention on something other

---

dealing with reality, not fiction" (ibid., 91). Enslin and Zeitlin represent most contemporary scholars when they judge that Torrey's argument that Bethulia is a pseudonym for Shechem is "scarcely definitive" (*Judith*, 80, n. 7). They point out that "Bethulia is high on the mountain; Shechem was not" (ibid.), and propose Beth-el as "an equally plausible guess" (ibid.). It seems best to leave the details of the Book of Judith alone as the products of a fertile, creative imagination. Much scholarly energy has been directed to finding the associations of the historical and geographical details of the book, and in every instance the arguments have proven themselves the products of the mind of the scholar.

[25]Of the little town of Bethulia, Metzger says, "It is passing strange that Bethulia, a city of such strategic importance, is otherwise unknown" (*Apocrypha*, 51). When all the data are assembled, there is virtually nothing about this little town that can be said with any certainty. Even its name is elusive. Bethulia can be translated on the basis of paranomasia or alteration as "House of God" (from *beth-el*), as "House of Ascents" (from *beth'eliya*), or as "Virgin" (from *bethula*). M. Gaster proposed this last interpretation in "Judith," *Encyclopaedia Biblica*, 1902, s.v., but it too has been rejected by most scholars. Alonso-Schökel points out that the Greek βαιτυλουα does not support this reading, though the Latin *Betulia* comes closer ("Narrative Structures," 19). Gaster had argued that the name *bethula* (virgin) was known from the Hebrew original, but of this claim Steinmann says, "Mais le mot *betoula* [*sic*] est absent du recit hebreu qu'il a publie" (*Lecture de Judith*, 44, n. 1). I prefer the translation "House of Ascents" as it picks up the emphasis on high places so otherwise prevalent in the story. It seems fitting that the town of the confrontation be located on a hill top. There is, of course, nothing more than preference to justify this interpretation.

[26]Dancy says of Part I that, "Its aim is to give a historical setting for the heroic deed, but it does so without the economy or the accuracy that a modern reader looks for" (*Shorter Books of the Apocrypha*, 6). It is precisely to the point that we cannot read Judith with "modern" expectations. To do so is to feel "deluded" (Alonso-Schökel, "Narrative Structures," 5) and "disappointed" (Brockington, *Apocrypha*, 44). The more I have worked with Part I as a literary/theological composition, the more I have become "enchanted" with its many layered proportions and points of contact. It is an ancient composition whose question "Who is your God" is strikingly modern.

than a historical recitation. If we were listening to the tale begun by Dentan or to the tale begun by Torrey, we would be alerted from the start, in a humorous fashion, to expect a message encoded in conflated details but in no way limited to them or by them.

The numerous geographical and historical absurdities of the opening sections of the Book of Judith should serve to alert us to listen closely for the point of the story. The carefully crafted repetitions delineated in the preceding discussion of these opening sections point repeatedly to the importance in the story of the one who claimed he was "the lord of all the earth," to the impeccable credentials backing his vainglorious claims, and to the foolhardiness of any who would go against the power of this leader. Nebuchadnezzar is established as an awesome ruler, imagined more powerful in this story than even the mighty Arphaxad in his incredibly well-fortified city of Ecbatana. And now this Nebuchadnezzar has turned his terrible wrath against those vassal nations who humiliated him when he called for their support. Holofernes has been commissioned to exact their humble submission.

PART I, SECTION THREE (2:14-7:32)

The remainder of Part I (2:14-7:32) develops the details of this enforced submission. The nations, one of which is Israel, are confronted with the costs of their foolish resistance. A three-fold chiastic pattern orders the tidy execution of Nebuchadnezzar's revenge as carried out by his henchman Holofernes: (1) A (2:14-3:10) and A' (7:6-32) are war stories that culminate in the desire to surrender; (2) B (4:1-15) and B' (7:1-5) are war preparations that include reference to Israel's great terror; and (3) C (5:1-6:11) and C' (6:12-21) are movements from the camp of Holofernes to the town of Bethulia through conversations with Achior. The symmetry and balance of the inner parallels in Section One and Section Two are continued here in the inner workings of the finely built proportions of a chiastic narrative structure. The upheaval of war, its preparations, and its effects are exquisitely controlled in the matching components of the story. The chaos of the content does not spill over into its form, though the narrative pace quickens with numerous alternations of national and geographical scene. The story flashes its camera first on one nation and then on another continually narrowing its focus from the nations of the world at large to the nation of Israel in particular and finally to a small town in this nation, Bethulia. A terrifying nightmare is enacted in which an enemy larger than life moves against a seemingly powerless little town, but this nightmare is kept within manageable bounds by a beautifully organized chiastic structure.

One of the most interesting compositional features of the first half of the story is the way in which one section of the narrative is linked to the next through verbal and/or serial concatenation.[27] In some instances, a striking word or phrase appears in successive sections. In other instances, identical or reversed series of events occur in successive sections of the story. For example, Section One is linked to Section Two through the repetition of the numeral "one hundred and twenty": Nebuchadnezzar rests for "one hundred and twenty days" (1:16) at the end of Section One; and in Section Two, he orders Holofernes to take "one hundred and twenty thousand foot soldiers and twelve thousand cavalry" (2:5) to atack the rebellious nations. In turn, Section Two is linked to Unit A (2:14-3:10) of the three-fold chiastic pattern which orders Section Three (2:14-7:32) by an identical numerical repetition: In Unit A, Holofernes "mustered the picked troops by divisions as his lord had ordered him to do, one hundred and twenty thousand of them together with twelve thousand archers on horseback" (2:15). In addition, the sequence of events in the A section mirrors a reverse image of the progression of events in the two opening sections: while Nebuchadnezzar rested with his troops for an extended period and then issued the order to muster the forces of retaliation, Holofernes first musters the forces and then settles down for an extended period of rest. In the opening section, after the defeat of Arphaxad, Nebuchadnezzar returns to Nineveh with his

---

[27]By concatenation, I mean the formal interlinkage of units within the narrative structure by means of repeated words or series of words that appear in strategic positions within the compositional units under consideration. I have avoided the description "key words" and its subdivisions "epiphora," the repetition of a word or phrase at the end of clauses, sentences, or verses; "anaphora," the repetition of a word or phrase at the beginning of clauses, sentences, or verses; and "anadiplosis," the repetition of the last word of one unit at the beginning of the next. These words are used most often to describe rhetorical relationships in successive units, which may or may not be related compositional units in the structure of the narrative. By concatenation, I mean to describe a compositional relationship in which units and sometimes sub-units are strung like matching beads on a chain. Concatenation bespeaks architectural similarity between the units which is based on a rhetorical relationship of repetition. On the usage and meaning of these terms, see Lanham, *Rhetorical Terms*, 44, 8, 7, respectively. For another interpretation of the compositional usefulness of these terms, see "Repetition as a Means of Linking Successive Episodes" in Rideout's "Prose Compositional Techniques in the Succession Narrative," 74-88. See also Shalom Paul, "Amos 1:3-2:3: A Concatenous Literary Pattern," *JBL* 80 (1961) 397-403.

troops and rests for one hundred and twenty days (1:16), and then he orders the collection of one hundred and twenty thousand plus soldiers (2:5). Inversely, in Unit A of the chiastic pattern, Holofernes first collects the one hundred and twenty thousand plus soldiers as ordered (2:5), and with them marches from Nineveh to the plain of Bectileth (2:21)—a three hundred mile journey which this numerous force manages in an incredible three days. Then Holofernes settles down with them for a one month stay (3:10). These identities in the series of events together with the verbal repetitions of the numeral one hundred and twenty give the beginning of the story a richly textured, interlocking quality. From the start, finely constructed concatenations in the narrative structure of Section One, Section Two and Unit A of Section Three set the tone of a well-told, carefully crafted story.

Throughout all of Part I (chapters 1-7), high places and the passes leading to them are of strategic importance. As with many of the details in the Book of Judith, the specific geographic locations mentioned in Part I are fantastic. The battle scenes are as geographically impossible as Nebuchadnezzar is historically impossible. Montague says, "The impossible zig-zagging of the campaign over the West simply sets the stage for the confrontation of a crushing world power with a people whose only power is faith in their Lord."[28] This is true, but the fact that the scene of the struggle between Assyria and those who challenge its supremacy is repeatedly on hill tops and mountain tops enhances the cultic aspect of this confrontation. The locus of enforced submission to Nebuchadnezzar as "god" is fittingly on high places.

The following summary of scenes and events in the major sections of Part I highlights the cumulative cultic effect hilltops and mountain tops have in the structure of the first half of the narrative.

Section One of the Introduction (1:1-16). Nebuchadnezzar engages in a war with his powerful political rival, Arphaxad, on the plain which is on the borders of Ragae (1:5). Nebuchadnezzar triumphs over Arphaxad, captures Ecbatana, and turns its "beauty into shame" (1:14).[29] Then Nebuchadnezzar finalizes his victory over Arphaxad in the "mountains" (τοῖς ὄρεσι) of Ragae, where he utterly destroys him with hunting spears (1:15).

---

[28]George T. Montague, *The Books of Esther and Judith* (New York: Paulist, 1973) 15-16.

[29]"Shame: (ὄνειδος) is sometimes political humiliation and sometimes religious humiliation. See the five appearances of the word in the Book of Judith: ὄνειδος in 1:14, 8:22, 9:2; ὀνειδισμὸν in 4:12 and 5:21.

Section Two of the Introduction (2:1-13). Interestingly, there are no cultic references or overtones in this passage. From his royal palace in Nineveh, Nebuchadnezzar issues the command for political revenge against the disobedient nations who disregarded his call for auxiliary troops in the battle against Arphaxad. His command calls for their submission to him as "the great king, the *lord* (ὁ κύριος) of all the earth" (2:5). He explicitly demands a show of subservience to himself as a political despot; he does not require the nations to bow to him as their religious god.

Section Three (2:14-7:32)—Unit A of the Chiastic Pattern (2:14-3:10). Holofernes' first military act of retaliation is against the "hill country" (τὴν ὀρεινήν, 2:22). After the surrender of the seacoast peoples who have seen the destruction wrecked on their neighbors, the text says of Holofernes, "Then he went down to the seacoast with his army and stationed garrisons in the 'hilltop cities' " (τὰς πόλεις τὰς ὑψηλάς, 3:6). From there, "He demolished all their boundaries (τὰ ὅρια)[30] and cut down all their sacred groves; for it had been given to him to destroy all the gods of the land, so that all nations should worship Nebuchadnezzar only, and all their tongues and tribes should call upon him as god (θεόν)" (3:8).

Unit B of the Chiastic Pattern (4:1-15). When the people of Israel hear what has happened to the holy places (τὰ ἱερά, 4:1) of their neighboring nations, they are greatly terrified. Their first act of defense is to seize "all the high hilltops" (τὰς κορυφὰς τῶν ὀρέων, 4:5). Joakim, the high priest (ὁ ἱερεὺς ὁ μέγας, 4:6)[31]

---

[30]τὰ ὅρια is sometimes translated as "high places" though elsewhere in the narrative it regularly is translated as "boundaries" or "borders" (1:10, 1:12, 2:25, 3:8, 15:5, 16:5. Cf. ὁρίοις in 1:5; ὅριον in 2:10, 4:4, 14:4, 15:4; and ὁρίων in 2:25). Enslin and Zeitlin note that both Fritzche and Ball are certain that τὰ ὅρια in 3:8 is a mistranslation of הבמות ("high places") and that this is reasonable considering the subsequent reference to "cutting down the groves" and "destroying all the gods" though "why the translator should have been confused is hard to say" (76, n. 8). It is not difficult to account for τὰ ὅρια as "boundaries" in 3:8 if Nebuchadnezzar's order that Holofernes capture πᾶν ὅριον αὐτῶν, "all their bounds" in 2:10 is recalled. In 3:8 as Holofernes moves beyond the directive issued by his lord in calling for acknowledgment of Nebuchadnezzar as God, it is entirely appropriate that the verse starts by echoing the very language of the order. That the political becomes religious is characteristic of the story.

[31]In Section B concern clusters around priestly matters. The fate of other places of sacrifice, τὰ ἱερά, 4:1, causes the high priest of

then orders them to defend "the passes up into the hills" (τὰς ἀνα-βάσεις τῆς ὀρεινῆς, 4:7).

Unit C of the Chiastic Pattern (5:1–6:11). When Holofernes hears that the people of Israel have closed the passes in the "hills" (ὀρεινῆς) and have fortified "all the high hilltops" (πᾶσαν κορυφὴν ὄρους) and set up barricades in the plains, he is very angry (5:1-2). He asks his generals about the identity of this people "in the hill country" (ἐν τῇ ὀρεινῇ, 5:3). Achior comes forward to tell the story of the people of "this hill country" (τὴν ὀρεινὴν ταύτην, 5:5) and of how they came into possession of "all the hill country" (πᾶσαν τὴν ὀρεινὴν, 5:15).[32] Holofernes is so displeased with Achior's words and with his suggestion that they pass by this nation, that he declares that Achior is to be bound and taken back into "the hill country" (τὴν ὀρεινὴν, 6:7). Thus Achior is led out to "the hill country" (τὴν ὀρεινὴν, 6:11) near the springs below Bethulia.

Unit C' of the Chiastic Pattern (6:12-21). Action narrows to the crest and the foot of the hill outside Bethulia and repeated phrases emphasize the narrowed scene of combat. The men of Bethulia, the town "on the crest of the hill" (ἐπὶ τὴν κορυφὴν τοῦ ὄρους, 6:12), take up their weapons and go out from Bethulia which was "on the crest of the hill" (ἐπὶ τὴν κορυφὴν τοῦ ὄρους, 6:12). The Assyrians slipping under "the hill" (τοῦ ὄρους, 6:13) fling Achior down at the base of "the hill" (τοῦ ὄρους, 6:13). The men of Bethulia rescue Achior and take him to the officials of the town.

Jerusalem, ὁ ἱερεὺς ὁ μέγας, 4:6, 4:8, 4:14 (cf. the only other occurrence of this designation in 15:8) to order a resistance. The religious transformation of an originally political confrontation is now entirely effected. Both the Assyrians led by Holofernes and the Israelites led by Joakim the high priest have acknowledged the true nature of their battle. The language of this section emphasizes that the continued existence of Israel's place of sacrifice is at stake.

[32]In Achior's speech (5:5-21), various forms of the word God appear twelve times (θεός in 5:9, 5:13, 5:17, 5:21; θεοῦ in 5:17, 5:18; θεὸν in 5:12, 5:19, 5:20; θεῷ twice in 5:8; and θεῶν in 5:8). For the most part these are references to Yahweh, the God of Israel. The word Lord appears only four times, and only one of these references is to Yahweh, "the Lord and God" (ὁ κύριος αὐτῶν καὶ ὁ θεὸς αὐτῶν, 5:21) of the Israel-ites. The other three occurrences of "lord" are part of Achior's political deference to Holofernes. His speech opens and closes with verbal bows to "my lord" (ὁ κύριός μου, 5:5 and 5:21). Included in his concluding comments is the acknowledgement of Holofernes as his "most sovereign lord" (δέσποτα κύριε, 5:20).

Unit B' of the Chiastic Pattern (7:1-5). The next day Holofernes breaks camp and moves against Bethulia by seizing the passes up into "the hill country" (τῆς ὀρεινῆς, 7:1). His armies encamp near the spring of Bethulia. When the Israelites see the vastness of the enemy armies, they despairingly declare that neither "the high mountains" (τὰ ὄρη τὰ ὑψηλά) nor the valleys, nor "the hills" (οἱ βουνοί) can bear the weight of such an enemy (7:4).

Unit A' of the Chiastic Pattern (7:6-32). On the second day Holofernes leads out his troops and examines the approaches to Bethulia. Some of his generals point out that the people of Bethulia rely not on spears for defense, but on the "height of the mountains" (ὕψεσι τῶν ὀρέων, 7:10) in which they dwell; they argue that it will be no light task to mount "to the crest of the mountains" (ταῖς κορυφαῖς τῶν ὀρέων, 7:10). And so they suggest that the water supply be cut off and the people be allowed to die of thirst. And so the vast Assyrian armies spread out to wait for their deadly plan to have its effect on the Bethulians. Meanwhile, after thirty-four days as captives in their own little town, the people of Bethulia gather around their leader and deplore their situation, declaring that "now we have no helper" (7:25). They want to surrender to the Assyrians, but Uzziah gets them to agree to hold on for five more days. Depression descends on the trapped people of Bethulia.

Activities on mountain tops are of undeniable importance in the Book of Judith. Nebuchadnezzar destroys his enemy Arphaxad in the mountains; Holofernes too moves against his enemies in the hills and hilltop cities, continually narrowing the scene of combat from hills in the large context of the "west" to a specific hill on which the town of Bethulia is built. While it is only to be expected that battles would be fought in hills, the interweaving of this imagery with the specific cultic notes about the destruction of places of worship (3:6-8), in spite of the prior surrender of these people (3:3) and the explicit fear of the people of Israel for their Temple in Jerusalem (4:2), transforms concern over the taking and defending of "hills" to concern over religious survival. Preservation of the holy becomes the real concern of these confrontations. Israel is set into action by the news of what happened to the "holy places" (τὰ ἱερά, 4:1) of its neighbors. Israel's defense is appropriately led by a great holy person, Joakim the high priest (ὁ ἱερεὺς ὁ μέγας, 4:8). What happens on one mountain top is linked to what may happen on another in the battle scenes of Part I (chapters 1-7). This concatenation of the scenes of conflict gradually builds in an increasingly terrifying crescendo of violence to the climactic confrontation on the Israelite mountain top city of Bethulia. Holofernes' proud boast, "Who is God except Nebuchadnezzar?" (6:2), voices the threat central to the story of the conflict told in the Book of Judith.

Violence marks all of the actions in Part I of the story. Assyria's aggressive acts of warfare and Israel's defensive acts of entrenchment and religious supplication are equivalent attempts at forceful manipulation.

PART I, SECTION THREE: UNIT A (2:14-3:10)

In Unit A (2:14-3:10) of the chiastic pattern of Section Three, there is an explosion of terms describing the physical violence of Holofernes' move against the nations. He "cut asunder" (διέκοψεν) Put and Lud (2:23); he "plundered" (ἐπρονόμευσεν) both the people of Rassis (2:23) and the sheep-folds of the Midianites (2:26); he "demolished" (κατέσκαψεν) the high cities along the Abron River (2:24); he "slew" (κατέκοψε) all the territory of Cilicia who resisted him (2:25); he "burned" (ἐνέπρησεν) the tents of the Midianites (2:26) and the fields of Damascus (2:27); he also "gave to des-truction" (ἔδωκεν εἰς ἀφανισμὸν) the flocks and herds of Damascus (2:27); he "sacked" (ἐσκύλευσεν) the cities (2:27) and "stripped bare" (ἐξελίκμησεν) the plain of Damascus (2:27); he "smote" (ἐπάταξεν) their young men with the sword (2:27); he "demolished" (κατέσκαψεν) all the boundaries of the seacoast cities (3:8), and "cut down" (ἐξέκοψεν) their groves (3:8), for it was given to him "to destroy" (ἐξολεθρεῦσαι) all the gods of the land (3:8). Two variations of the verb κόπτω ("to cut") and two occurrences of the verb κατασκάπτω ("to demolish") frame this peric-ope of violence: διέκοψεν and ἐξέκοψεν appear respectively in 2:23 and 3:8, κατέσκαψεν appears in both 2:24 and 3:8.[33] Unit A delineates a

---

[33]Enslin and Zeitlin summarize the dispute over the meaning of the phrase κατέσκαψεν πάντα τὰ ὅρια ("he demolished all their borders," 3:8). Some scholars see τὰ ὅρια as a mistranslation of הבמוֹת ("high places"). While this is in parallelism with the cultic imagery in the second half of the verse in which groves are cut down, the argument is not without its difficulties. Enslin and Zeitlin take issue with it by citing other instances and uses of τὰ ὅρια in scripture (p. 76, n. 8). However, τὰ ὅρια also appears in Jdt 2:25, thus the phrase is loosely a part of the chiastic frame around the pericope (διέκοψεν, 2:23; κατέσκαψεν, 2:24; τὰ ὅρια, 2:25; τὰ ὅρια, 3:8; κατέσκαψεν, 3:8; ἐξέκοψεν, 3:8). I describe the inclusion of τὰ ὅρια as loosely a part of the pattern because another verb does intervene in 2:25 before its appearance. While I cannot on structural grounds resolve the question of the translation of τὰ ὅρια in 3:8, I believe it is important to be mindful of its appearance at the beginning

pool of terms for physical violence which climaxes in the destruction of the gods of the land.

PART I, SECTION THREE: UNIT B (4:1-15)

In Unit B (4:1-15) of the chiastic pattern of Section Three, Israel under the direction of the Jerusalem High Priest Joakim[34] forcefully counters the threat of Assyrian violence with acts of two kinds: (1) they take possession of the narrow passes into the cities atop the hills of Judea (4:4-7); and (2) they perform numerous acts of public supplication of God (4:8-15). The actions of Unit B are direct results of what the people of Israel have heard about the aggression of the Assyrians. In a way not specified in the story, the Israelites "hear" (ἤκουσαν, 4:1) that Holofernes has "sacked" (ἐσκύλευσεν, 4:1; cf. 2:27) all the shrines of their neighbors and has "given them over to destruction" (ἔδωκεν αὐτὰ εἰς ἀφανισμόν, 4:1; cf. 2:27). This linkage of passages by means of "hearing" what has happened in the other camp is the first occurrence of a pattern that marks the remainder of Part I where each of the shifts of scene in the chiastic pattern opens with a reaction either to hearing about what the enemy party has been doing or eventually to seeing the actions of the enemy party first hand. This Assyrian aggression initiated in Unit A (2:14-3:10) sets into motion an interconnected three-fold chiastic action-reaction sequence (A-B-C-C'-B'-A') first bonded by the "hearing" described in the opening verse of Unit B (4:1).

Unit B continues with an explosion of acts of religious supplication that parallels the explosion of military acts of aggression in Unit A. The people of Israel pray "in great earnestness" (ἐν ἐκτενείᾳ μεγάλῃ, a phrase twice repeated in 4:9). And with a great use of "sackcloth" (σάκκους, thrice repeated in 4:10, 11, 12), they cover virtually everything

---

of the pericope where it does not carry the meaning of "high places." In addition, τὰ ὅρια also appears in 1:10 and twice in 1:12 where it again does not carry the meaning "high places." However, τὰ ὅρια appears in 15:5 and 16:4 and in both instances the meaning "high places" would be appropriate: "Damascus and its high places" (15:5) and "burn up my high places" (16:4). Interestingly, a form of κόπτω (ἔκοπτον), one of the other words in the frame around the violence pericope in Part I, makes its only other appearance in the Book of Judith in 15:5.

[34]The proportions of this confrontation are drawn with tangents to the worst experiences of the people of Israel, thus setting the stage for a resolution that will exceed the dimensions of any difficulty the people could ever imagine facing.

in sight including men, women, babies, cattle, sojourners, slaves, and the
altar itself, praying that "their inheritance not be given to destruction" (εἰς
ἀφανισμὸν, 4:12; cf. 4:1). They fast (4:13); they offer burnt offerings and
vows as freewill gifts (4:14); they put ashes on their heads and cry continually to God (4:15). In short, they hope by these acts to escape Assyrian
domination.

PART I, SECTION THREE: UNIT C (5:1-6:11)

In Unit C (5:1-6:11) of the chiastic pattern in Section Three, the scene
shifts back to the Assyrian camp where in an unspecified way it is "reported"
(ἀνηγγέλη, 5:1) to an angry Holofernes that the people of Israel have
prepared for war. He calls together the Canaanite leaders and asks them a
series of five questions (5:3-4): (1) who are these hill people, (2) what cities
do they inhabit, (3) what is the size of their army and in what does their
power or strength consist, (4) who is their king and leader of their army, and
(5) why have they refused to surrender?

These questions occasion Achior's coming forward to recite the history of Israel from the time of the patriarchs to the time of the return to
Jerusalem after the exile (5:5-21). In this lengthy speech he tells Holofernes
that these are people descended from the Chaldeans (5:6), and that they
inhabit "all the hill country" (5:15, 19) because of the actions of their God.
Indeed, their strength rests in this powerful God and in their faithfulness to
this God. If they sin, they are punished.[35] If they do not sin, then their God
will defend and protect them to the defeat and shame of the Assyrian army
(5:21).

These words enrage the other officers and they protest that they "are
not afraid" of the Israelites (5:23). They want to fight and Holofernes
agrees. He chastises Achior (6:2-9), saying, "And who are you, Achior?" to
dare such blasphemous claims. Holofernes declares that there is no god
except Nebuchadnezzar (6:2), and condemns Achior to share the fate of the
Israelites. Thus Achior is deposited at the spring beneath Bethulia.

PART I, SECTION THREE: UNIT C' (6:12-21),
UNIT B' (7:1-5), UNIT A' (7:6-32)

The actions of the remainder of Section Three in Unit C' (6:12-21), Unit
B' (7:1-5), and Unit A' (7:6-32) move quickly. With the exception of the last

---

[35]On this passage as an interpretation of the exile, see Haag, *Judith*,
32.

verses of Unit A', all the actions of these sections are clearly consequent to matters defined in the preceding sections. In Unit C', Achior "tells" (ἀπ-ήγγειλεν, 6:17) the Israelites about Holofernes' boasts against the house of Israel, with the result that the Israelites renew their supplication of their God (6:18, 19, 21b). In Unit B', Holofernes moves his huge army into the valley beneath Bethulia (7:1-3), with the result that the terrified Israelites, seeing their vast numbers, cry out all the louder to their God (7:4-5). In Unit A', Holofernes parades around the city and eventually decides to destroy the people of Bethulia by cutting off their water supply (7:6-18). Now comes the surprise that even though the people of Bethulia cry out to their God, their courage fails (6:19ff.). After a period of thirty-four days, they murmur against their leaders and demand that Bethulia be surrendered to the As-syrians (7:19-28). Uzziah responds with a brief but devastating reply: give God five more days to help us, then we will surrender (7:30-31). Section Three of Part I ends with the dismissal of the men of Bethulia to their posts, and the women and children to their homes. All are greatly depressed (7:32). Ironically, the fortified passes have held, but their loudly proclaimed reliance on God has crumbled.

By the end of Part I, two important thematic ideas have been played in counterpoint against each other in episodes involving Assyria or the na-tions at large and in episodes involving Israel or specifically the town of Bethulia: (1) mountain tops have been the scenes of military confrontations and of cultic strivings for survival; (2) violence of first a military sort and then of a religious sort has aimed at ensuring supremacy of allegiance to the most powerful God.

"Fear" runs throughout Part I as a *leitmotif* interlinking these two im-portant thematic ideas. The struggle began because the nations "did not fear" (οὐκ ἐφοβήθησαν) Nebuchadnezzar and dared to send his envoys for auxiliary troops back empty-handed (1:11). This misjudgment was punished by the destructive retaliation led by Holofernes, which caused "fear and trembling" (φόβος καὶ τρόμος, 2:28a) to fall on the seven cities of Sidon and Tyre, Sur, Ocina, Jamnia, Azotas, and Ascalon so that they "feared him greatly" (ἐφοβήθησαν αὐτὸν σφόδρα, 2:28b).[36] The news of the

---

[36]The locations of these cities are geographically difficult. The seacoast cities of Sidon, Tyre, Azotus (equals Ashdod), Ascalon are listed from north to south in proper order. But Jamnia is nine miles north-northeast of Ashdod, while Sur and Ocina are otherwise unknown. Some scholars hold that Sur is Dor, a port near Carmel and that Ocina is Acco, a city north of Dor. On these matters, see Friedrich Stummer, *Geographie des Buches Judith* (Stuttgart: Kath. Bibel-Werk, 1947) 28.

disasters which have befallen their neighbors effects "very great fear" (ἐφοβήθησαν σφόδρα σφόδρα, 4:2) of Holofernes in Israel too. They are
"terrified" (ἐταράχθησαν, 4:2) for the safety of Jerusalem. The Assyrians
protest that they "do not fear Israel" (οὐ γὰρ φοβηθησόμεθα, 5:23).
And finally, when Israel sees the Assyrian host, they are "greatly terrified"
(ἐταράχθησαν σφόδρα, 7:4), and declare that their deep ravines and high
mountains will simply not be able to bear the weight of such an enemy.

PART II, SECTION A (8:1-8)

Episodic concatenation continues as Part II opens with the notice that
Judith "heard" (καὶ ἤκουσεν, 8:1). Before she even appears in the story,
we know that she knows what Uzziah and the people of Bethulia have agreed
to do. Section A (8:1-8) of the chiastic pattern which orders Part II[37] of the
narrative does not detail the specifics of what she has heard, but rather
continues immediately with "a quick sketch of her life."[38] Action is sus-
pended until 8:9 when the verb "and she heard" will be repeated and followed
by the description of what she heard. The first three verses of the introduction tell about Judith's father (8:1) and about her husband (8:2-3). The next
five verses of the introduction tell about Judith's manner of life as a widow
(8:4-8).

Judith is the daughter of Merari who is the son of the fourteenth
generation of descendants of Jacob (8:1). The genealogy is actually the
genealogy of her father, and all of the forefathers of her father are listed by
name in 8:1. While it would seem unwise to make too much of this genealogy, since most of the names that appear in it have proven imaginary,[39] it is

---

While I cannot resolve the issue of geographical location here, I do note
that there are seven cities listed and that this may be significant. Jdt 2:28
is framed by notices of fear with the words καὶ ἐπέπεσεν φόβος καὶ
τρόμος opening the verse and the words ἐφοβήθησαν αὐτὸν σφόδρα
closing it. That seven cities are listed may signify that fear was fully and
completely felt by the nations alongside Israel.

[37]See the diagram of the external structure of Part II on p. 62-63.

[38]Enslin and Zeitlin, Judith, 109, n. 8.1.

[39]I agree with Enslin and Zeitlin's argument that since the tale of
Judith is "the product of the story-teller's imagination rather than of the
historian's memory, any serious treatment of the genealogy is wasted effort"
(p. 110). Arguing along these same lines M. Steinmann, in Lecture de Judith
(Paris: J. Gabalda et Cie, 1953), points out that the fictitious names in the
genealogy have been borrowed from Numbers 1:6, 8 and 26:8, 57 and from

significant that Judith has the longest genealogy attached to her name of any woman in the Hebrew Bible.[40] Judith whose name literally means "Jewess" is the daughter of Merari (1. son of Ox, 2. son of Joseph, 3. son of Oziel, 4. son of Elkiah, 5. son of Ananias, 6. son of Gideon, 7. son of Raphaim, 8. son of Ahitub, 9. son of Elias, 10. son of Chelsias, 11. son of Eliab, 12. son of Nathaniel, 13. son of Salamiel, 14. son of Sarasadai), a descendant of Israel himself. Interestingly, Judith's name like that of her distant ancestor Israel is both the name of a people and the name of an individual who plays a significant role in the life of the people bearing this name.

Following a note about her husband's death and burial (8:2-3),[41] the narrative specifies that Judith has been living as a widow "for three years and four months" (8:4). It may be coincidental that Judith's credentials occur in multiples of seven, but it is nonetheless true that she is of a family two times seven generations removed from Jacob and that she has been living as a widow for three years and four months. It is equally true that the author of Judith has already demonstrated a tendency to inventive manipulations of figures (see the use of "one hundred twenty" in the opening chapters of the book) prior to these notes about Judith.

Judith's introduction continues with details about her present way of life that link her practices to important images already developed in Part I.

Nehemiah 12:12-21 (pp. 72-73). Steinmann suggests that the purpose of the genealogy is to make Judith a Samaritan (p. 72) and to mock the aristocrats of the author's day who forged pedigrees (p.74). Going beyond these sorts of interpretations of the genealogy in Jdt 8:1, J. Edgar Bruns, in "The Genealogy of Judith" (CBQ 18:1 [1956]), argues that the genealogy supports his hypothesis that "Judith is none other than the Jael of Jgs 4-5 transformed first by the colonists at Elephantine and later by the Jews at Leontopolis into a heroine whom we know as Judith" (p. 19). Bruns uses the genealogy to support a historical date for the book of 146 B.C.E. and a setting for its author of Leontopolis (pp. 20-22).

[40]So Dancy, Shorter Books of the Apocrypha, 95.

[41]The details of Manasseh's death are frequently likened to the story of the death of the Shunamite woman's son in 2 Kings 4:8ff. It is true that the woman and her husband have a small room built on their roof for Elisha (4:10) and that Judith lives in a small room on the top of her house (8:5). It is also true that Manasseh dies from sunstroke while out in his fields during the barley harvest (8:2-3), and that the Shunamite's son is struck ill while in the field with the reapers and with his father (4:18). But there is no more than superficial similarity between the story of the Shunamite woman and the story of Judith.

Judith lives on a mountain top of sorts, in that she has constructed a tent for herself on the roof of her house (8:5). She wears sackcloth (8:5), and she fasts every day except those feastdays on which fasting is not permitted (8:6). Most importantly, she is known in her community as one who "feared god exceedingly" (ἐφοβεῖτο τὸν θεὸν σφόδρα, 8:8). Verse 7 inserts the information that Judith is a beautiful and wealthy woman, maintaining the large estate left her by her dead husband Manasseh. Thus in vv. 4-8 of the introduction, Judith is portrayed as a woman who understands the proper use of high places, the right practice of piety, and the true basis of "fear." Judith is a widow, a woman alone in a story where only other men in her life and her community bear names. She has no children, she is beautiful, and she is wealthy. Her strength and her reputation rest in her personal holiness: "No one spoke ill of her, for she feared God exceedingly" (8:8). With this last note, her introduction is complete and the story which has been held in abeyance to establish these credentials for her now continues.

PART II, SECTION B (8:9-10:9a)

Section B (8:9-10:8) resumes with the reiteration of the words "and she heard" (καὶ ἤκουσεν, 8:9), this time continuing with the specifics that she has heard of the wicked words of the people and of the compromise struck by Uzziah. Hearing of these things, Judith sends the woman in charge of her household[42] to summon the officials of Bethulia for an accounting. This meeting between Judith and the town officials is one of the most memorable and most important exchanges in the book. Dancy rightly claims that the theology presented in Judith's words here rivals the theology of the Book of Job.[43] Judith unequivocally declares God's purposes cannot be bound by human designs. The scene in the tent atop her house is one both profound and comic. That the three officials drop everything and come to the house of this pious widow for a sound upbraiding is a marvelously

---

[42]Judith's servant is most often designated by the word ἄβρα in the text (8:10, 33; 10:2, 5; 13:9; 16:23), which means "favorite slave" (Liddell and Scott, *Greek-English Lexicon*, 3). Elsewhere in the text, this woman is designated by the more usual servant words παιδίσκη (10:10) and δούλη (12:15; 13:3). The woman does not speak in the story, but she does have an intimate relationship with Judith. Judith's first and last actions in the story involve her: in 8:10 Judith sends her "favorite slave" to summon the officials of Bethulia; in 16:23, Judith's last action before the notice of her own death is to set her "favorite slave" free.

[43]So Dancy, *Shorter Books of the Apocrypha*, 70, 99.

incongruous occurrence in a story as thoroughly male dominated as is the story of the Book of Judith.

Episodic concatenation continues in Section B as the things that Judith has heard now impel her to declare that the officials "hear" her words, and to beg that God "hearken to" her plea. The section is composed of three sub-sections and a brief introduction and conclusion:

Introduction (8:9-10)

Judith "heard" (ἤκουσεν) and sent her maid to summon the town officials.

Meeting (8:11-36)

Judith and the officials speak together:

a. Judith declares, "Listen to me!" ('Ακούσατε δή μου). You have put God to the test, when it is we who are being tested (8:11-27).

b. Uzziah responds by excusing their behavior and asking her to pray for rain (8:28-31).

c. Judith declares again, "Listen to me!" ('Ακούσατέ μου). She says she has a plan whereby Israel will be delivered by her hand and tells them to meet her later that same evening by the city gate (8:32-34).

d. Uzziah and the officials bless her and return to their posts (8:35-36).

Prayer (9:1-14)

Just at the time of evening when prayers are being offered in the Jerusalem Temple, Judith turns to God and begs that her voice be heard, "O God, my God, listen to me a widow" (εἰσάκουσον ἐμοῦ, 9:4). She recites past acts of God's protection and begs the Lord who crushes wars to give her the strength to do what she plans. "By the deceit of my lips strike down the slave with the prince and the prince with his servant; crush their arrogance by the hand of a woman" (9:10). She concludes, "God of my Father and God of the inheritance of Israel . . . listen to (εἰσάκουσον) my entreaty" (9:12).

Preparation (10:1-5)

She dresses in her most beautiful apparel and prepares a travelling bag of ritually pure food which she gives to her maid.

Conclusion (10:6-9a)

Judith and the maid go to the city gate where they meet the town officials. Her change in appearance impresses the officials who pray that God will bless her (10:7-8). The simple note that she worshiped God completes the section.

Of particular charm in this section is the continued use and development of forms of the verb ἀκούω. The introduction, the meeting, and Judith's prayer stress the importance of listening. The modulation from the Aorist indicative "she heard" (ἤκουσεν, 8:9) to the Aorist imperative command "hear me" (ἀκούσατε, 8:11, 32) to the Aorist imperative request "listen to me" (εἰσάκουσον, 9:4, 12) accents Judith's understanding of the importance of hearing and of demanding to be heard. Once her prayer is finished, so too is the use of the verb ἀκούω in this section. With resolve both Judith and the story move forward.

Judith's words to the officials (especially 8:11-27) and to God (9:1-14) are composed of arguments based on present and past experiences. Dancy points out that her long speech to the officials breaks into two sections which address first the problem of faith (8:12-17) and then the question of suffering (8:18-27). He maintains that "these are the two themes of the book of Job, and in this passage the author of Judith can stand comparison with the author of Job."[44]

In the first section of her speech (8:11-17), Judith declares that what the officials have done is wrong. She challenges their actions with an interrogative phrase reminiscent of the words Holofernes used to upbraid Achior. Judith says to the officials, "Who are you to test God?" (τίνες ἐστὲ ὑμεῖς οἳ ἐπειράσατε τὸν θεόν, 8:12). Earlier Holofernes had said, "Who are you, Achior" (τίς εἶ σύ, 6:2) to encourage us to avoid a conflict with the people of Israel? Later in the story, Judith herself in response to an invitation to a party in the tent of Holofernes will say to his servant, "Who am I to refuse my master?" (τίς εἰμι ἐγώ, 12:14). These phrases function to chastise: Judith clearly means to admonish the officials of Bethulia for exceeding the rightful limits of their authority; similarly, Holofernes meant to challenge Achior's boldness; and eventually, Judith will employ the phrase as a pun that underscores the Assyrian's arrogance and utter ignorance of her understanding of exactly who she was and of precisely who her *true* master was. In the instance of her words to the officials of Bethulia (8:12), Judith accuses them of putting themselves in the place of God. In the context of citing their inability to plumb the depths of the human heart (8:14), she asks them how they dare to think they can search out the ways of God. Her words bespeak a radical faith grounded on the hard insistence that God has the power to protect or even to destroy (8:15).[45]

---

[44]Dancy, *Shorter Books of the Apocrypha,* 99.

[45]Judith plays out her whole story with the kind of faith described in the Prologue of Job (esp. 1:21 and 2:9). Her faith is like that of Job after his

Central to her argument and in many ways descriptive of the story itself are her words:

> Do not try to bind the purposes of the Lord our God; for God is not like a man to be threatened, nor like a human being to be won over by pleading (8:16).

The Assyrians threatened to secure their supremacy; the Israelites pleaded with God by fasting, praying, and ritually covering themselves and their surroundings with sackcloth to achieve security. Here Judith declares that God is a God not to be coerced. Faith means "waiting for deliverance" (8:17) which may or may not come. Faith is known in the quality of the waiting, not in the reality of destruction or deliverance.

In the second section of her speech to the officials (8:18-27), Judith reminds them that their generation has not sinned by knowing other gods, therefore they can hope that God will not disdain them (8:18-20). She points out that capture would mean the destruction and plunder of the sanctuary (8:21) and that slavery would mean dishonor (8:23). Therefore, she urges the officials to set an example for the townspeople (8:24). She argues that God is putting *them* to the test (ὃς πειράζει ἡμᾶς, 8:25). She closes her speech with the reminder that tests were faced by Abraham, Isaac, and Jacob (8:26), saying,

> For he has not tried us with fire,
>   as he did them to search their hearts;
> and he has not taken vengeance upon us,
>   rather for their admonition does the Lord
>   scourge those who draw near to him (8:27).

Enslin says of this passage,

> In this climax to her speech Judith gives expression to what may be styled the saving confidence of Judaism, seemingly evidenced so clearly throughout her history. Through the fires of adversity God was perfecting his chosen people, was subjecting them to constant and bitter punishment, but with the purpose of fitting them for their glorious destiny.[46]

Unifying Judith's words in both the first and second parts of her speech is the conviction that to God alone belongs the right to test. The officials

---

experience of God in the whirlwind (cf. 42:1-6), yet in the story she has no special theophanic experience. We can only imagine what happened on her housetop where she was habitually a woman of regular prayer.

[46]Enslin and Zeitlin, *Judith,* 118-19, n. 27.

have "tested" God (ἐπειράσατε, 8:12) by "trying" (ἐξετάζετε) the Lord Almighty (8:13). But Judith argues that it is God who is "trying" them (πειράζει, 8:25), just as Isaac was "tested" (ἐπείρασεν, 8:26) and just as the hearts of their forebears were put to the "fiery test" (ἐπύρωσεν εἰς ἐτασμὸν, 8:27). Judith calls for a reversal in their thinking, but the officials do not hear her. Instead, Uzziah asks her to pray for rain (8:31). Judith responds with the imperative, "Listen to me!" (8:32). She says that she will meet them at the town gate that night, and within the days in which they have said they would hand over the city, the Lord will look with favor on Israel in an action accomplished by her hand. She refuses to detail her scheme, and the officials do not press her. They bless her and return to their stations.

At this point in the story all the significant elements of the confrontation have been played out. The question about who is the true God and the issue of what does faithfulness to this God require have been sketched in full opposition. In the name of serving God, three alternatives have been suggested: (1) threatening by aggression, (2) pleading by prayer, and (3) serving by letting go of success or failure. The remainder of the story is the resolution of these alternatives.

Judith has called for a reversal on the part of those who have tested God. She has urged them to realize that they are the ones being tested. Now, in her prayer (9:1-14), she cries out in a loud voice to God (9:1), just as her community had done when first confronted with the threat of the Assyrians (4:9). Imperatives of supplication begging God "to listen" (εἰσάκουσον, 9:4 and 9:12) appear at strategic points in her entreaty. Invoking God who enabled her ancestor Simeon[47] to take revenge on the enemies who defiled his daughter (9:2-4a), she implores, "O God, my God, listen to me also, a widow" (9:4b). In a beautifully constructed temporal chiasmus which stretches from the remote past to the remote future, she acknowledges that all things are in the foreknowledge of God (9:5-6). To "the Lord who crushes wars" (9:7), she addresses a five-fold request (9:9-11a):

> Look on their arrogance,
> Send your wrath on their heads,
> Give into my hand—the widow's—the strength for that which I
>   have proposed,

---

[47]Simeon is not mentioned in Judith's genealogy in 8:1. Here the reference is to the story of Dinah's violation and defense in Genesis 34.

> Smite slave—by the guile of my lips—with prince
>   and prince with his servant,
> Break into pieces their high estate by the hand of
>   a female,   ⎤ chiasmus
>   ⎦
>   For not in numbers is your power
>   nor is your might in men of strength.   ⎤ chiasmus
>   ⎦

Then in a litany (9:11b-12) composed of ten titles for God, five on each side of the words ναί ναί, which climaxes with the request that God "hear" her entreaty, Judith praises God as the God of the humble, the helper of the oppressed, the one who upholds the weak, the protector of those in despair, and the savior of the hopeless. Following the strong affirmation, "yea, yea," or "verily, verily," she continues to praise God as the God of her ancestors, the God of the inheritance of Israel, ruler of heaven and earth, creator of the waters, and king of all creation. She concludes her prayer with the explicit request that her "word and deceit be for the wound and bruise of those who have purposed hard things" against Israel (9:13),[48] so that all nations and tribes may know the power and might of God who alone is the one shielding the people of Israel (9:14).

  This passionate and finely said prayer is a full chapter long. Both its length and its carefully shaped petitions make clear Judith's care about her request. She wants God's power to be made manifest to all nations and tribes; she wants the Assyrians brought low; and she intends to accomplish all this by "the guile of her lips" (9:10) and by her "word and deceit" (9:13). The defeat she plans is an ignominious one; she wants to "break in pieces their high estate by the hand of a *female*" (9:10). Here in 9:10 and again in 13:15 and 16:5, the author uses the word θήλεια in place of the more regularly employed γυνή.[49] In all three cases, the author emphasizes that "by the hand of a female" Yahweh triumphs.[50]

---

[48]Four times in her prayer Judith employs forms of the word "deceit" (ἀπάτη). In a difficult phrase at the opening of the prayer, she recalls that the rulers who violated her ancestors were slaughtered and their bed, "which was ashamed of the deceit they had practiced" (RSV translation of τὴν ἀπάτην αὐτῶν ἀπατηθεῖσαν εἰς αἷμα, 9:3) was stained with blood. Again in 9:10, she asks that "by the deceit" (ἀπάτης) of her lips the enemy be smitten. And in 9:13, she asks that her word and "deceit" (ἀπάτην) bruise the enemy.

[49]According to Enslin and Zeitlin, "The use of θήλεια in place of γυνή is deliberate; it adds to the extraordinary victory of Judith and to the disgrace of the defeated foe" (*Judith*, 125, n. 10).

[50]For further development, see Patrick W. Skehan, "The Hand of Judith," *CBQ* 25 (1963) 94-109.

Once finished with her prayer, Judith moves into action. Her immediate preparations involve first the adornment of herself (10:3-4) and then the preparations of ritually pure food for the trip (10:5). The author delights in the details of her adornment, literally from head to toe. This sequenced physical description of Judith's dressing includes her bathing,[51] anointing her body with precious ointment, fixing her hair, and dressing gaily. She puts on sandals, anklets, bracelets, rings, and earrings.[52] And she does all this "to deceive" (εἰς ἀπάτησιν) the eyes of those who will behold her (10:4).[53] Next she gathers together ritually pure food and utensils to use on her journey. She hands these to her favorite maid and they go forth to meet the town officials.

She has done her work of preparation well and the officials, including Uzziah, Chabris, and Charmis—who are here mentioned for the last time in the story as a threesome (10:6)[54]—marvel at her beautiful transformation

---

[51] That there was no water in the town of Bethulia is of no concern to the author at this point in the story.

[52] Sequenced physical descriptions are known by the genre designation *wasf*. Notable parallels appear in a seven-fold description of the beauty of the beloved in the Song of Songs (4:1-7) and in an eleven-fold description of Sarai's beauty in the Genesis Apocryphon (20:2-6). In each instance the woman's beauty is enticingly described and erotic delight seems to be the intention of the passages. See Roland Murphy, "Form Critical Studies of the Song of Songs," *Int* 27 (1973) 418-20. Cf. also Solomon Zeitlin, "The Dead Sea Scrolls," *JQR* 47 (1957) 253.

[53] The author is untroubled by the ethical concerns of modern commentators. In this life and death situation, Judith unambiguously sets out "to deceive" the enemy. The story has been called "somewhat shocking" (Dentan, *The Apocrypha*, 61), "fierce and almost vindictive" (Metzger, *Apocrypha*, 52), and has been accused of containing "some distinctly revolting passages" (Oesterley, *Apocrypha*, 176), one of which is Judith's prayer in 10:3-4. For another defense of her actions, see Dubarle, "Légitimité de la ruse de Judith," *Judith*, 1.166-69.

[54] Uzziah, Chabris, and Charmis' names are mentioned together only three times in the story. In 6:15, they are mentioned together as the rulers of the city of Bethulia. In 8:10, Chabris and Charmis are summoned by Judith's favorite maid to come to the meeting at her house (Uzziah's name is mentioned in 8:9 and he speaks in 8:28, indicating that he is in attendance at the meeting even though not specifically mentioned in 8:11). In 10:6, the threesome bless Judith and pray that God grant her success on her journey. Chabris and Charmis appear nowhere else in the story—their function is secondary—though their appearance at the beginning and end of Section B (8:9-10:8) frames this unit within the story.

(10:7). They pray that God will grant her success (10:8), and she too worships God (10:9a). Thus ends Section B of Part II (8:9-10:9a).

This lengthy and important section of the story continues the kind of intricate linkage of narrative units that we have observed elsewhere in the story. This section is confined to the city limits of Bethulia and defined by the appearance of Uzziah, Chabris, and Charmis at its opening and closing. Threaded throughout the unit are concern for Jerusalem/Zion, Judith's desire to "deceive" (ἀπατάω), concern that her words be "heard," belief that deliverance will be "by her hand," and emphasis on the fact that she is a woman and a widow. The following summary highlights these and other repetitions within the various parts of this unit:

Section B—A Scene in Bethulia: Judith Plans to Save Israel (8:9-10:9a)

A. Judith Summons the Town Officials (8:9-10)
  (1) Judith "heard" about the compromise and sent her maid to summon Uzziah, Chabris, and Charmis
B. Exchange between Judith and the Town Officials (8:11-35)
  (1) Judith upbraids the officials
    (a) "Hear me"—you have "tested" God (8:11-17)
    (b) God is "testing" us (8:18-27)
  (2) Uzziah replies (8:28-31)
      Your words are true and your wisdom well-known, but pray for rain (8:28-31)
  (3) Judith responds (8:32-34)
      "Hear me"—I have a plan and within the days after which you promised to hand over the town, the Lord will deliver Israel "by my hand"—stand at the city gate tonight
  (4) Uzziah and the officials take their leave (8:35-36). They pray that God will grant her success
C. Judith's Prayer (9:1-14)
    At the very hour when the evening incense is being offered in Jerusalem, Judith cries out to the Lord (9:1)
  (1) To the God of her father Simeon, who protected Israel in the past, "smiting" slaves, princes, and rulers on account of one so "deceived," she begs, "O God, my God, 'hear' me also, a 'widow' " (9:2-4)
  (2) In an intricate temporal chiastic bridge between the preceding memory and her subsequent request, she acknowledges that all things past and future are in God's foreknowledge (9:5-6)
  (3) She lays the present distress with the exalted Assyrians before the Lord who "crushes" wars, asking that they who intend to defile the

sanctuary be brought low. She, a "widow," asks for the strength to do what she purposes. By the "deceit" of her lips, she asks that slaves, princes, and servants be "smitten," and that their arrogance be broken "by the hand" of a woman (9:7-10)

(4)   She praises God with a series of ten titles, begging that the Lord "hear" her entreaty and make her words and "deceit" bring down those who are against the covenant and against the crest of Zion, so that all will know that God alone protects Israel (9:11-14)

D. Judith's Preparation (10:1-5)
Judith calls her maid and goes down into her house (10:1-2)

(1)   She makes herself beautiful so as "to deceive" all who see her by taking off her sackcloth and "widow's" garments and putting on her most festive attire (10:3-4)

(2)   She prepares ritually pure food and utensils for her journey (10:5)

E. Judith Meets with the Officials (10:6-9a)

(1)   Uzziah, Chabris, and Charmis who are waiting at the gate for Judith, marvel at her beauty and then pray that God will grant her success. Judith worships God.

PART II, SECTION C (10:9b-10)

Section C (10:9b-10) functions as a bridge between the longer and more complicated B and D Sections. Section C is set apart by reason of its being a scene between these two other scenes, by its being a time for a change of sets from that of Bethulia to that of the Assyrian camp, and by virtue of its having a mirror section (13:10b-11) in which the major components of this section are repeated in reverse order. Here in 10:9b-10, Judith asks the elders to order the gates opened for her. When the young men have opened the gates, Judith and her maid go forth. As the men watch, the women go down the mountain and pass straight through the valley to where the Assyrians are encamped. Their three steps: (1) out the gate, (2) down the mountain, (3) through the valley, take them directly into the camp of the enemy.

PART II, SECTION D (10:11-13:10a)

In Section D (10:11-13:10a), Judith will overcome the enemy as personified by Holofernes, but not without a considerable building of tension and suspense, as the five days in which she has to accomplish her deed evaporate one by one with little or no seeming change in the situation. This, of course, is the heart of the story structurally and that part of the story which has been immortalized, as Ruskin says, by "about a million vile pictures."[55] The actual murder of Holofernes is quickly told at the finish of the scene with the Assyrians. Judith is alone with Holofernes during this final part of the scene for a total of ten verses (13:1-10). He sleeps the whole time, and she prays twice (13:4-5 and 7) before striking his neck twice with his own sword (13:8). This account of the murder, rendered in a single verse, is the incident for which the Book of Judith is famous.

Section D (10:11-13:10a) is a relatively straightforward section in which Judith systematically sets about "deceiving" all who meet her. She does precisely what she said she would do in her prayers (cf. 9:10, 13), and what she set out to do by dressing in finery (10:4): she "deceives" (ἀπατάω) the Assyrians. Her words in this section are sometimes true in the literal sense (cf. 11:10), sometimes true in the sense of having double meanings (cf. 11:6), and sometimes outright lies (cf. 11:8).[56] Her actions, however, are

---

[55]Ruskin, "Mornings in Florence," 335.   Judith, the slayer of Holofernes; Jael, the slayer of Sisera; and Tomyris, the slayer of Cyrus are counted in art as the female "types" who prefigure the Virgin Mary's triumph over Satan. On the allegorical and stylized treatments of these subjects in paintings, see Robert W. Berger, "Ruben's 'Queen Tomyris with the Head of Cyrus,' " *Bulletin of the Museum of Fine Arts Boston* 77 (1979). From the lavish illustrations in this article, it is readily apparent that artists have repeatedly used the pose of the woman on the left and the male victim on the right of the picture in a position beneath her. Berger is unable to account for this repeated positioning of the figures, but the reproductions are nonetheless fascinating.

[56]In his "Critique of Luis Alonso-Schökel on Judith," Shumaker expresses dissatisfaction with Judith's lies. He says, "I should prefer Judith not to speak outright falsehoods for roughly the same reason that I should not like Kissinger to bring about the end of the oil embargo by lying" (p. 33). In responding to Shumaker, Alonso-Schökel defends Judith by a lengthy discussion of the ambiguity of passages containing reference to κύριος where she means God and Holofernes understands something else. Alonso-Schökel concedes that Judith does lie when she speaks about clean and unclean (pp. 48-49). Shumaker replies that he still has "compunctions about her methodology" (p. 50). Then Dundes, another respondent, jumps into the discussion and adds that he "can't think of a single folk hero or heroine who doesn't use some form of deceit" (p. 51). All of these comments overlook Judith's prior statement in her prayer that she was going to use "deceit" to overcome the enemy. She first says she will use deceit, and then does so. Thus in those passages where she lies, she is being true to her own words. In 9:10 and 13 when she says she wants to overcome the enemy by ἀπάτη, there is no other interpretation except that she plans to use a trick, fraud, deceit, guile, or treachery (see Liddell and Scott, *Greek-English Lexicon*, 181).

consistently true to her religious ideals: she eats only pure food (12:2-4, 19), she prays with her habitual regularity (11:17; 12:6; 13:3-4, 7), and she bathes daily to maintain her ritual purity (12:7).

Delays in terms of threes retard the actions in this section. Judith meets first with the Assyrian patrol (10:11-17), second with the Assyrian camp (10:18-19), and third with Holofernes (10:21ff.). After her one conversation with Holofernes (10:20-12:4) and its follow-up, message-sending exchange in which she secures the permission to leave the camp for daily prayer and bathing (12:5-7), "three days" pass in which nothing seems to happen.

Repeatedly, this section stresses that the actions occur at night (νύξ): 11:3, 5, twice in 11:17; 12:5, 7. And repeatedly, the section emphasizes that all who meet Judith marvel at her beauty and wisdom:

1. The patrol "marvel at her exceeding beauty" (θαυμάσιον τῷ κάλλει σφόδρα, 10:14).

2. The Assyrian camp "marvel at her beauty" (ἐθαύμαζον ἐπὶ τῷ κάλλει αὐτῆς, 10:19).

3. Holofernes and his attendants "marvel at the beauty of her face" (ἐθαύμασαν πάντες ἐπὶ τῷ κάλλει τοῦ προσώπου αὐτῆς, 10:23).

4. After her first speech (11:5-19), Holofernes and his attendants "marvel at her wisdom" (ἐθαύμασαν ἐπὶ τῇ σοφίᾳ αὐτῆς, 11:20). They comment, "There is not such a woman from one end of the earth to the other for beauty of face and understanding of words" (ἐν καλῷ προσώπῳ καὶ συνέσει λόγων, 11:21).

Because he was greatly impressed by Judith's beauty, Holofernes determined to have intercourse with her (12:12, 16). Throughout Section D he is biding his time, awaiting the moment when he can "deceive" her (ἀπατῆσαι, 12:16). Thus Judith and Holofernes are players at the same game; she is there to "deceive" the Assyrians and bring about their demise; he is waiting for the day when he can "deceive" her and bring about her disgrace. She praises his "wisdom" (σοφίαν, 11:8); he marvels at her "wisdom" (σοφίᾳ, 11:20).[57] In the end, Judith proves the more skillful. Her wisdom is indeed a marvel, and her deceit a complete success.[58]

---

[57]The word σοφία appears only three times in Judith. Prior to these two instances in 11:8 and 11:20, Uzziah had acknowledged to Judith that all in Bethulia knew of her "wisdom" (8:29).

[58]In *Judith*, Haag suggests that Judith mocks Holofernes in 11:5-9 in her ironical deception. She makes a "false oath to a false God" ("zum falschem Gott fugt sie den falschen Schwur," p. 48); she mocks the false

Section D (10:11-13:10a) contains the following units of material:

I.   Initial Meetings (10:11-12:4)[59]
   A. Judith Meets the Patrol (10:11-17)
       Judith tells them that she is a daughter of the Hebrews on her
       way to meet Holofernes in order to show him a way to capture
       the hill country without losing a single man.[60] The patrol
       marvel at her beauty and tell her not to be afraid; then they
       choose one hundred men to escort her to the tent of Holofernes.
   B. Judith Meets the People of the Camp (11:18-19)
       The news of her arrival causes a great stir and the people come
       out to see her. All marvel at her beauty, saying, "Who can
       despise this people, who have women like this among them?
       Surely not a man of them had better be left alive, for if we let
       them go they will be able to ensnare the whole world!"
   C. Judith Meets with Holofernes and his Servants (10:20-12:4)
       (1) Introduction (10:20-23)
            Holofernes is in his tent resting on his bed, under a
            canopy. He and his servants come to the front of the
            tent to meet Judith, and they all marvel at her beauty.
       (2) Holofernes speaks to Judith (11:1-4)
            Holofernes tells her to take courage (11:1 and 3) because
            he has never hurt anyone (11:1 and 4) who chose to serve
            Nebuchadnezzar.[61]

---

self-image of her opponent just as the Lord mocks the arrogance of the
haughty Assyrians in Isa 10:13. He argues that irony in 11:2-23 is unmis-
takable, that Judith makes a fool of Holofernes so that this episode becomes
"like a parable" ("gleichnishaft," p. 50).   Judith's actions take on this
parabolic character since her story shows how Yahweh will judge the
heathens who oppose the people of Israel (cf. p. 52).

[59]Note that the three initial meetings follow the same pattern: Judith
meets a group, they marvel at her beauty, and a touch of humor concludes
the meeting. The patrol choose one hundred men to help her to the tent; the
camp decides that a people who could produce a woman the likes of her
could "ensnare the whole world"; and Holofernes wonders about her food
supply only to have Judith assure him that she has enough to last until "the
Lord by my hand accomplishes what he has purposed."

[60]Cf. 7:11 where Holofernes' own men suggest this same idea.

[61]Holofernes seemingly forgets for the moment that he destroyed the
cultic sites of the seacoast peoples who had already surrendered to him (cf.
3:1-8).

(3)   Judith replies to Holofernes (11:5-19)

She promises to tell her lord nothing false that night and proceeds to tell him that God is going to accomplish his purpose through him. She acknowledges Nebuchadnezzar as king of all the earth, and admits to having heard about Holofernes' wisdom and skill. Then she reminds him of Achior, and declares that Achior spoke the truth. She tells him that the people of Israel are about to commit a terrible sin because of their great hunger. She explains that she is a God-fearing woman who will know the moment of her people's sin and will tell Holofernes when he can safely go against the people of Israel and capture Jerusalem.

(4)   Holofernes compliments her and orders a meal for her (11:20-12:4).

Holofernes and those with him marvel at her wisdom. He says that God has done well in sending her into their hands. He commands that a meal be prepared for her, but she declines his offer. He wonders how she will survive after her own food runs out, but she assures him that she will not use up her things until the Lord accomplishes by her hand what he has purposed.

II.   The Passing of Time in the Assyrian Camp (12:5-9)

A.   Judith is taken to a tent where she sleeps until midnight. She awakens and sends a message to Holofernes requesting permission to go out of the camp to pray. He commands the guards not to hinder her and for the next three days she remains in her tent, except for a routine late night bath, prayer, and nightly meal.

III.   The Party (12:10-13:10a)

A.   The Invitation and Preparation (12:10-15)

On the fourth day, Holofernes desiring to have intercourse with Judith, sends his eunuch, Bagoas, to invite her to a party. Bagoas invites Judith to share an evening meal in Holofernes' tent where she will make merry and become as a daughter of the children of Asshur. Judith says, "Who am I to refuse my lord," and agrees to come. She dresses in her best finery and has her maid prepare a meal and a place for her in the tent of Holofernes.

B.   The Feast (12:16-13:10a)

   (1)   The First Part of the Evening (12:16-20)

Holofernes is in ecstasy at the sight of Judith, for he is very anxious to have intercourse with her and has been waiting for the proper moment when he can deceive her. He says, "Drink and make merry." She says, "Indeed, yes, my lord, I will drink, because my life has been exalted today to a height beyond that of all the days since my birth." Then she eats and drinks the food her maid has prepared for her. He is so enraptured that "he drank exceeding much wine, more than he had ever drunk in one day since he was born."

   (2)   The Second Part of the Evening (13:1-10a)

Everyone makes haste to withdraw from the tent because the hour has grown late. Only Judith and Holofernes are left. Judith had already instructed her maid and Bagoas that she will later go out of the camp as was her daily custom. Holofernes is overcome with all he has drunk and is asleep on his bed. Judith stands beside him and prays that God will grant her success for the exaltation of Jerusalem. Next she goes to the bedpost and takes Holofernes' own sword, prays again, and strikes his neck twice. She rolls his body from the bed and takes its canopy down. She gives the head and the canopy to her maid who puts them in the food bag, then the two of them leave the camp.

In addition to the intention of Holofernes to "deceive" Judith, an intention whose language is drawn from her prayer,[62] Section D also derives a great deal of its language from preceding scenes. Especially noteworthy among these parallels are the following:

(1)   Men marvel at Judith—Uzziah expresses respect for Judith's wisdom (8:29); and later the three town officials of Bethulia marvel at her beauty (10:7). In contrary order, the Assyrians first marvel at her beauty (10:14, 19, 23; 11:21), and then express respect for her wisdom (11:20).

(2)   Fear and its opposite, courage—Throughout Part I, fear was an exceedingly important aspect of the story. Now in Section D, the

---

[62]See the discussion on pp. 90-91.

Assyrians repeatedly urge Judith to have no fear and to take courage (10:16; 11:1, 3). But Judith says she is God-fearing (11:17).

(3)   The question of personal identity expressed by the formula, "Who are you?" or "Who am I?", appears on the lips of Holofernes against Achior (6:2); on the lips of Judith against the officials (8:12); and in Section D on the lips of Judith in response to the party invitation (12:14).

(4)   The question of the identity of the true God—Holofernes' brave words that only Nebuchadnezzar is God (3:8; 6:2) are mocked by his words to Judith in 11:23, "If you do all you have said, your God will be my God, and you will sit in the house of King Nebuchadnezzar."

(5)   Concern for Jerusalem—Whereas in 4:2, 12; 8:21, 24; and 9:8, 13 there is concern for the safety of the sanctuary and for keeping the Assyrians away from Jerusalem, in 11:19 Judith promises to help Holofernes establish his dominion in the very midst of this city.

The richly textured quality of Section D derives from its many points of contact with the other sections. Section D does indeed contain many enchanting passages; however, praise for this section should properly be shared with the other parts of the story. Thus I find that I must disagree with some of Alonso-Schökel's comments on this section:

> With chapter 10 begins what some critics consider the center of the story. This center is no doubt the best part and a masterpiece of narrative art in Hebrew literature. It is this section which gives greatness to the book, fame to its author and popularity to the story among readers, writers, and artists.[63]

In the story, Section D is structurally the heart of the chiastic pattern which organizes Part II. It is distinguished by virtue of both its structure and its content, but its greatness must be shared with the rest of the story. There is a resolution, albeit a private one, in this section of the dilemma which threatened Israel. Judith knows that her people are saved, but she has still to make this news known to her community.

PART II, SECTION C' (13:10b-11)

Section C' (13:10b-11) functions as a bridge between the D and B' Sections. This section is again a scene which allows a set change, this time

---

[63] Alonso-Schökel, "Narrative Structures," 5.

from the Assyrian camp back to the town of Bethulia. Judith and her maid reverse the three steps they took on their initial journey as now they go (1) through the valley, (2) up the mountain, and (3) approach the gate. Judith cries out in a triumphant little hymn:

> Open, open the gate!
> God, our God is with us
>   to show yet again
>   his strength in Israel and
>   his might against the enemies,
>   even as he has done this day (13:11).

PART II, SECTION B' (13:12-16:20)

In Section B' (13:12-16:20), God's triumph through the hand of Judith is made public. The section moves quickly in an antiphonal fashion, alternating moves in the sequence of events from Judith's return, to the plundering of the Assyrian camp, to the triumphant entry into Jerusalem, with moments of prayer.

The scene climaxes with a long hymn of praise (16:1-17) which celebrates Judith's triumph in much the same way that the hymns in Exodus 15 and Judges 5 celebrate the events of the crossing of the sea and the victory of Deborah and Barak.

The major contours of Section B' can be sketched as follows:

I.   In Bethulia (13:12-14:11)
     A. Public Announcement of Her Triumph (13:12-14)
         (1)   Amazed that she has returned, all the people of Bethulia run to the gate where they kindle a fire for light and gather to hear her news.
         (2)   She proclaims in a loud voice,

> "Praise God—Praise—Praise God,
>   who has not withdrawn his mercy
>   from the house of Israel,
>   but has destroyed our enemies by my
>   hand this night."

     B. Public Display of Her Trophy (13:15-17)
         (1)   Judith takes the head of Holofernes out of her bag and shows it to the people, assuring them that her honor was left intact but that God struck down this hated enemy "by the hand of a woman."[64]

---

[64]In Greek ἐν χειρὶ θηλείας, which is the same expression used in 9:10.

(2) The people bow down and "bless"[65] God who has this day brought their enemies to naught.

C. Uzziah Applauds Judith's Triumph (13:18-20)

(1) Uzziah "blesses" Judith as beyond all women on earth, and he "blesses" God as the creator. He declares that Judith's hope will remind all of the strength of God. He asks that God make her deeds a perpetual exaltation because she did not spare even her own life to avenge their fall.[66]

(2) The people affirm his prayer with the words, "Amen, amen."

D. Judith's Plan (14:1-5)

(1) The familiar imperative, "Listen to me,"[67] opens Judith's instruction to the people that they take Holofernes' head and hang it on the city wall. She instructs them to wait until morning, and then to rush the Assyrian camp, so that the tables will turn and "fear" will overcome the Assyrians. But first, she wants Achior the Ammonite brought to her so that he can see the head of the man who had sent him to his death.

E. Achior's Conversion (14:6-10)

(1) Achior is brought into the assembly, and when he sees the head of Holofernes he falls down. He is raised up only to fall a second time at Judith's feet. He, like everyone else

---

[65]The word εὐλογέω appears only seven times in the Book of Judith, and all of its occurrences are in Section B'. In 13:17, the people bless Judith; in 13:18, Uzziah blesses Judith and then blesses Yahweh; in 14:7, Achior blesses her; in 15:9, the high priest Joakim and the Jerusalem council all bless her; in 15:10, they ask the Lord to bless her forever; and finally in 15:12, the women of Israel bless Judith.

[66]In Greek εὐλογητὴ σὺ θύγατερ and εὐλογημένος κύριος (13:18). Enslin and Zeitlin remark that this "non-Greek construction (εὐλογητὴ + dat.)" reflects the Hebrew of the blessing of Abraham by Melchizedek (Gen 14:19), the blessing of Ruth by Boaz (Ruth 3:10), and the blessing of Jael by Deborah (Jud 5:24). See their discussion in *Judith*, 155-56, n. 18.

[67]Cf. 8:11, 32, Judith's chastisement of the officials of Bethulia. She also uses the words in her prayer before beginning her journey to the Assyrian camp (cf. 9:4, 12).

in the episode, declares her "blessed" (εὐλογημένη) and says that those in every nation who hear her name will be terror-struck. Then he asks her to tell all that happened to her in the Assyrian camp.

(2)   In a one verse narrative notice, the story records that she told everything that had happened since the moment of her departure from Bethulia.

(3)   In response to her tale, the people raise a great shout and make a joyful noise. Achior, seeing all that God has done, believed firmly in God and was circumcised and joined the house of Israel.[68]

F.   The Departure for the Assyrian Camp (14:11)

(1)   At dawn, the head of Holofernes is hung on the wall of Bethulia and the men take up their weapons and go out in companies to the passes in the mountains.

II.   In the Assyrian Camp (14:12-15:7)

A.   The Discovery of Holofernes' Death (14:12-15:2)

(1)   The Assyrians see that the people of Bethulia are preparing for war and order Bagoas to awaken Holofernes.

(2)   Bagoas goes to the tent of Holofernes and calls since he assumes Judith is there. When no one answers, he goes into the bedchamber where he finds Holofernes dead, with his head missing. He runs outside and shouts, "The

---

[68]Achior's admission into the community of Israel flies in the face of the prohibition in Deut 23:4 unless this prohibition is read literally, "No Ammonite or Moabite shall enter the assembly of the Lord; even to the tenth generation none belonging to them shall enter the assembly of the Lord for ever; because they did not meet you with bread and water on the way, when you came forth out of Egypt, and because they hired against you Balaam the son of Beor from Pethor of Mesopotamia, to curse you." Since Judith is more than ten generations removed from Jacob (8:1), it could be argued that Achior is more than ten generations away from the Ammonites and Moabites who mistreated the Israelites. However, this argument is strained and I know of no one who puts it forward. Achior simply remains a mystery. For a good summary of what is said about him, see Steinmann's chapter on Achior in *Lecture de Judith,* 55-62. He concludes that it is indeed a scandal that Achior is made the only true believer with Judith, that he is circumcised, and that he becomes a member of the community. But Steinmann argues that there are other scandals in this story when you begin to read between the lines. For instance, "A quelle race appartiennent les magistrats et le peuple de Bethulie?" (p. 62).

slaves have tricked us! One Hebrew woman has brought
disgrace on the House of King Nebuchadnezzar! Behold,
Holofernes on the ground, and his head is not on him!"
(14:18)

(3) When the leaders of the Assyrians "heard this,"[69] they
were aghast and cried out loudly.

(4) When the men in the tents "heard it," "fear and
trembling"[70] fell on them and they fled.

B. The Attack (15:3-7)

(1) The men of Israel rush on the fleeing Assyrians.

(2) Uzziah sends men to the surrounding area to tell what has
happened. Then they all fall on the Assyrians in a great
slaughter. The Israelites plunder the Assyrian camp,
taking possession of its riches.

III. First in Bethulia and Then in Jerusalem (15:8-16:20)[71]

A. The Jerusalem High Priest and the Council Come to Praise
Judith (15:8-10)

(1) Joakim the high priest and the Jerusalem council[72] come
to see the good deeds which the Lord has done for Israel
and to hail Judith. When they meet her they all "bless"
her for ever.

(2) All the people second their prayer: "Amen."

B. An Interlude (15:11)

(1) The people plunder the Assyrian camp for thirty days.
They bring Judith all the rich trappings from the tent of
Holofernes and she loads everything on her mule.[73]

---

[69]In the beginning, when the people of Israel "heard" about
Holofernes' attacks, they too were greatly terrified. Cf. 4:1.

[70]The phrase τρόμος καί φόβος appears twice in Judith. Here
in 15:2, the Assyrians experience what they caused in 2:28.

[71]The location for 15:8-10 is not specified in the story. But Bethulia
can be assumed since Joakim comes to see Judith and she has not left the
town since she returned (13:11).

[72]On this "council," mentioned in 4:8, 11:14, and 15:8, see Enslin and
Zeitlin, *Judith*, 81-82, n. 8. On the basis of this council and the high priest
with political authority in Jerusalem, a mid-second century date is often
proposed for Judith (see Pfeiffer, *New Testament Times*, 295).

[73]The text reads τήν ήμίονον, "mule" in the singular. This may
be a touch of humor, since the load is excessive for one animal. Could it be
that Judith's female donkey, like Judith herself, can do what it usually takes
a team to do? Of course, there may simply be a mistake in the text; several
manuscripts do substitute the plural.

    C. On to Jerusalem (15:12-16:17)

        (1)   The procession (15:12-13)[74]

            All the women of Israel gather and "bless" Judith. Wearing olive branches, they lead a dance, waving branches and singing songs of praise. The men, garlanded too, follow the women in a dance as they process to Jerusalem.

        (2)   The hymn of triumph (15:14-16:17)

            Judith leads the people in a triumphant song.

        (3)   Celebration in Jerusalem (16:18-20)

            All worship and offer freewill gifts to God. Judith dedicates everything that the people had given her, as well as the canopy from the bed of Holofernes which she had taken for herself. The people continue a three-month celebration in Jerusalem and Judith remains with them.

Judith's hymn of praise in chapter 16 merits close attention. The question still remains whether the Book of Judith developed out of the poem or whether the author of Judith included the poem following the models of other liberation stories which climax in song like "The Song of the Sea" (Exodus 15) or "The Song of Deborah" (Judges 5). At the outset, let me say that I cannot resolve this question though I suspect that the song was included in the original composition of the story.[75]

Judith 16 fulfills a liturgical function in the story. Its introductory verse tells that Judith sang this song and that all the people echoed her words of praise (15:14). The scene suggests a liturgical procession of the people on their way to Jerusalem (cf. 16:18). The song celebrates Yahweh's victory by alternating confessional words of praise with narration describing God's saving deed and Judith's courageous action. It is a liturgical song with

---

[74]Cf. Exodus 15:20 and Isa 30:29 where dancing accompanies a pilgrimage celebrating liberation.

[75]Literature on Judith 16 is limited primarily to commentaries. See, however, H. Ludin Jansen, "La composition du Chant de Judith," *AcOr* 15 (1937) 63-71. This is a dated article in which Jansen proposes a three-part structure for the song: 16:1-4 is isolated as a unit because it contains motifs found regularly in thanksgiving psalms; 16:5-12 is isolated on the basis of containing the legend of Judith; and 16:13-17 is described as a unit with the character of a hymn like those used for accession to the throne. These units are not defendable on the basis of more natural content breaks. However, Jansen's argument that "la forme actuelle du psaume est purement litéraire" (p. 71) is an intriguing one.

several parts, and we can well imagine—taking the hint from the introductory statement that Judith sang and the people sang other parts—that this is a song of active participation. It is, of course, impossible to know exactly who sang which part, but taking the lead from the text itself about the structure, the following scheme suggests itself.

A. Hymnic Introduction (16:1-2)

1. Introit (16:1)—Judith calls the people to worship

> Strike up a song to my God on timbrels,
> Sing unto the Lord with cymbals,
> Raise for him a psalm and a tale of praise,
> Honor and invoke his name.

In the first two lines, symmetry is achieved through three synonymous sets of parallel terms. In the second two lines, symmetry is achieved through a grammatical balance of noun plus noun and the similar construction of imperative plus imperative (ψαλμὸν καὶ αἶνον, ὑψοῦτε καὶ ἐπικαλεῖσθε).

2. Confession (16:2)—Judith declares the basis of her triumph

> For Yahweh is a God who crushes wars!
> For into his camps in the midst of his people[76]
> He has delivered me from the hand of those who pursued me.

Judith acknowledges God in the language of her prayer in 9:7 as the one who συντρίβων πολέμους, as the one who has personally delivered her from her pursuers. The word ὅτι, functioning like the climactic כִּי in Hebrew, appears at the beginning of the first two lines of this unit. This repetition adds to the drama and excitement of Judith's proclamation that Yahweh is a mighty warrior.

B. Narration of the Epic Event (16:3-12)

1. Judith tells of the Assyrian threat (16:3-5)

> Came the Assyrian from the mountains of the north,
> Came his armies with the ten thousands of his host,
> Whose multitude stopped up the valleys,
> And whose horsemen covered the hills.

---

[76]This portion of 16:2 is notoriously difficult; see Enslin and Zeitlin, *Judith*, 169, n. 2. Some manuscripts give the reading, "He has set up his camp among his people."

> He said he would burn my borders,
> (And) my young men slay with the sword,
> (And) my infants dash to the ground,
> (And) my babies take as booty,
> (And) my maidens he would despoil.
> The Lord Almighty has thwarted them by the hand of a female!

The remarkable rhythm of this section is difficult to capture in translation, though even here the exposure of ἦλθεν at the beginning of the first two lines, and αὐτῶν in the next two lines, followed by the quick succession of καὶ plus a noun, plus μου in the remainder of the passage can be sensed. The terror of Part I (chapters 1-7) is once again brought to mind, though here in a poetic fashion. Judith speaks in maternal language with the succession of possessive pronouns accenting her involvement in the intended devastation. The passage ends with the triumphant confession that Yahweh foiled the enemy through the hand of a female (cf. 9:10; 13:15).

2.   A description of Judith's triumph (16:6-10)

In the following section, Judith no longer speaks in the first person; rather her great deed is described by another voice. Possibly another member or portion of the group participating in this liturgical song recited these verses:

> For not did their champion fall by the hand of a young man,
> Nor did the sons of the Titans smite him,
> Nor did tall giants set upon him;
> But Judith, the daughter of Merari,
> By the beauty of her face undid him.
> For she put off her widow's dress,
> To raise up those in distress in Israel.
> She anointed her face with perfume,
> She bound her hair with a headband,
> She took a linen dress to deceive him.
> Her sandal ravished his eye,
> Her beauty made captive his heart;
> The sword passed through his neck.
> Persians shuddered at her daring,
> And Medes at her boldness
>   were terror-struck.

Picking up Judith's claim in 16:5 that God had triumphed through the hand of a "female," this section details exactly how the triumph was accomplished. Dancy points out that only in this section is there specific reference to the deed of Judith. He suggests that though this section may have been the "original core" of the song, it "is now worked up so much that it cannot convincingly be dissected."[77] The section delights in the unexpected nature of Judith's conquest. Three negative clauses build up to the fact that Judith with her beauty undid the enemy. Her beauty, metaphorically speaking, is her weapon or her "sword." And the climactic line, "the sword passed through his neck," can be read both literally as the weapon cut off his head and figuratively as he "lost his head" over the beauty of Judith. The effect of her deed is that the Persians and the Medes are terrified. Though the enemies are Assyrian, they are not mentioned here. The final word of the passage is that the Medes were "terror-struck."[78]

3.   Judith tells how her people rallied to destroy the Assyrian army (16:11-12)

> Then my humble ones raised their shout of triumph,
> And my weak ones uttered their cry;
> And (the enemy) were filled with dismay.
> They raised their voices and were turned in panic.
> The sons of maidens pierced them through,
> And wounded them like the children of fugitives;
> They perished before the army of my Lord.

In response to the people's account of Judith's mighty deeds, here Judith herself tells how their fear was transformed into courageous actions. Before the sons of women who were themselves still maidens, the Assyrian army perished.

C.   Hymnic Response (16:13-17)—Judith and the Community Sing a Song of Praise

The singular possessive pronoun "my" in 16:13 and 16:17 indicates that these words belong to Judith. The intervening verses of the passage could be a corporate response to her call to "sing a new song to God" (16:13; cf. 16:1). Since Judith has responded to praise of her deeds before with a prayer (cf. 10:9), it would be in keeping with her usual behavior for her to do so here. Of course, the entire passage could have been sung by Judith, but the following sharing of its parts is also possible.

---

[77] Dancy, The Shorter Books of the Apocrypha, 125.

[78] "Terror-struck" (ταράσσω) is used regularly in the story. Aorist forms appear in 4:2 and 7:4 to describe Israel's fear of the enemy, and in 14:19 and 16:10 to describe the enemy's fear of Israel. A future passive form appears in 14:7 where Achior predicts what will happen to the nations who hear of Judith's great deed.

1. Judith praises God with a new song (16:13)

> I will sing a new song to my God a new song.
> Lord, great are you and glorious,
> Marvelous in strength, invincible.

Just as many had "marvelled" (θαυμάζω) at her beauty and wisdom (10:7, 19, 23; 11:20), now Judith "marvels" at the glorious power of Yahweh.

2. The people join Judith's song of praise (16:14-16)

> Let all your creation serve you;
> Because you did speak, and you were made.
> You sent forth your spirit, and it formed them.
> And there is none who can resist your voice.
> For the mountains will be shaken from their foundations
>   with the waters,
> Rocks before your face will melt like wax;
> But to those who fear you, you will show mercy.
> For no sacrifice is sufficient to please you with its fragrance,
> And all fat for a whole burnt offering is to you exceedingly small;
> But the one who fears Yahweh is forever great.

Here Yahweh is hailed in cosmic terms that recall the language of Judith's requests in her first prayer, that God be known as "ruler of the heaven and the earth, creator of the waters, king of all creation" (9:12). In a real way, the sentiment of this passage expresses a resolution to the story of the Book of Judith. Now the people know that Yahweh, not Nebuchadnezzar, is the true "king of all the earth."[79] Now they know that right "fear" (φοβουμένοις, 16:15; φοβούμενος, 16:16) of the Lord is the ground of a proper relationship with God. And now they know that their God is not a God to be manipulated with acts of piety.[80]

---

[79] See the discussion of Nebuchadnezzar's claim on pp. 67-69.

[80] I agree with Enslin and Zeitlin's comment: "Attempts to read into these lines a minimizing of acts demanded by the law are quite unwarranted in the light of Judith's almost excessive care for their fulfillment" (*Judith*, 174, n. 16). I read these lines not as a prophetic-like disparagement of cultic practices, but as a reminder that excessive piety cannot be used to manipulate Yahweh. The verse accents "fear of the Lord." In a story where fear was misplaced and sackcloth, ashes, and offerings were overdone, this reminder about what is "little" in the eyes of the Lord is entirely appropriate.

3.   A closing admonition in which Judith expresses confidence in God's power (16:17)

> Woe to the nations which rise up against my people!
> The Lord Almighty will punish them on the day of judgement;
> To give their flesh fire and worms,
> And they will wail forever alive to the pain.

The imagery of this closing passage is sometimes described as a witness to the developing ideas of eschatology.[81] I agree with Enslin and Zeitlin that the imagery here seems more like a "rhetorical flourish of heightening of phrases long familiar"[82] than a break with orthodoxy. The prayer ends on a confident note in which Judith warns any who might rise against her people to take warning that her God is the Lord Almighty who is forever great.

    With the preceding divisions of voices, chapter 16 can be outlined as a two-part psalm in which the first part sets out the reasons for the singing, and the second part is itself the new song. Part I opens with Judith's declaration that "a psalm and a tale of praise" (ψαλμὸν καὶ αἶνον, 16:1) should be raised to the Lord, and Part II opens with Judith's announcement that now she is indeed singing "a new song" (ὕμνον καινόν, 16:13) to her God. Her sections of the chapter have been determined by the appearance of first person pronouns (I/my); the sections of the chapter belonging to other members of her community have been determined by natural breaks in the content and by third person narration about Judith's deeds. The following scheme summarizes the preceding discussion of chapter 16:1-17.

Part I
    A. Hymnic Introduction (16:1-2)
        1.   Introit (16:1)—Judith calls the people to worship
        2.   Confession (16:2)—Judith declares that Yahweh is the basis of her triumph

---

[81]See especially, Steinmann, "Judith Éternelle," in *Lecture de Judith*, 129-35, where he argues that this story is a synthesis of two genres, "la *haggada*, heritage des Sages et la vision apocalyptique, dernière forme de la prophetie" (p. 129). I find his arguments forced, but they represent an approach followed by many. On internal grounds, the interpretation of Judith and Holofernes as characters representing God and Satan, and of Judith as an emulation of "la femme couronnée de douze entoiled de l'*Apocalypse*, la communauté de l'éternel Israel de Dieu en lutte mortelle avec le dragon" (p. 134) is insupportable.

[82]Enslin and Zeitlin, *Judith*, 175, n. 17.

B. Narration of the Epic Event (16:3-12)
1. Judith tells about the Assyrian enemy (16:3-5)
2. The people (?) tell how Judith undid the enemy (16:6-10)
3. Judith tells how her people rallied to destroy the Assyrian army (16:11-12)

Part II

C. Hymnic Response to Praise (16:13-17)
1. Judith marvels at the strength of Yahweh by singing a new song (16:13)
2. The people join Judith's song of praise (16:14-16)—they demonstrate a new understanding of right fear of the Lord and proper worship
3. A closing admonition (16:17)—Judith expresses confidence in God's power

The two-part structure of this song and its climactic declaration in the people's part of the new song that a right understanding of "fear of the Lord" is the ground of true greatness and unshakable security is so closely related to both the form and the content of the preceding chapters of the Book of Judith that it is unlikely, in my opinion, that this closing hymn was written by any hand except that responsible for the preceding story. The most likely model for this hymn seems to be The Song of the Sea. Judith 16 and Exodus 15 are remarkably similar in terms of function, form, and content.[83] Both are liturgical songs that celebrate the triumph of Yahweh at the end of a longer narrative unit. Both alternate passages in which the leader speaks in the first person with passages in which another voice narrates the deliverance that has been effected for the people. Both speak of God as a divine warrior (notably, Jdt 16:2 and Exod 15:3) and as the creator. And in both, there is confidence that with Yahweh there need be no fear. It seems most plausible to me that the author of Judith followed the model of the Exodus story[84] in ending his story in a way similar to the way in which the ancient

---

[83]For particulars about Exodus 15, see Muilenburg, "A Liturgy on the Triumphs of Yahweh," 233-51. He analyzes the composition of this hymn as an A-B-C sequence in which each section divides into a hymnic confession, an epic narrative, and a hymnic response, Encircling this sequence is a hymnic introit and a closing hymnic acclamation.

[84]Skehan is more confident than I am of this parallel. He says unambiguously, "There is no doubt as to what is the poetic prototype for the canticle of Jdt: it is the canticle at the Exodus (Ex. 15, 1-19) connected with the name of Miriam" ("The Hand of Judith," 96). See his comparison of

author of Exodus had chosen to end that particular portion of the Book of Exodus.

PART II, SECTION A' (16:21-25)

In Section A' (16:21-25), the narrative slips into third-person description of particulars about the remainder of Judith's life. Thus Part II of the Book of Judith ends as it began with a description of the woman called Judith. Here at the end of the story, it says that she lived in Bethulia (16:21), that she remained a widow even though many desired to marry her (16:22),[85] that she became more and more famous and reached the age of "one hundred and five years."[86] Her last act before her death was to free her favorite maid (ἄβραν, 16:23). This unnamed woman is with Judith to the end of the story. Just as Judith's first act was to send her to summon Uzziah, Chabris, and Charmis, now her last act is to free her (16:23). Judith distributes her wealth to her kin before her death. Israel mourns the loss of Judith for seven days (16:24). And the story closes with the note, "There was no longer any who spread fear (ἐκφοβῶν)among the children of Israel throughout the days of Judith and for many days after she had died" (16:25).

Exodus 15 and Judith 16 on pp. 96-98 of this study. In his review, "A. M. Dubarle, O.P., *Judith: Formes et sens des diverses traditions, Tome I: Etudes, Tome II: Textes,*" 347-49, Skehan adds, "Be it then stated here more plainly than was done in *CBQ* 25 (1963) 108, that the Book of Judith has a central and controlling theme, to which all else is subordinate: it is a conscious and systematic meditation on the providence of God for Israel, prepared as a *haggadah* for Passover; the invisible hand of God, and the hand of Moses at the Exodus, are reflected in the deed wrought by the hand of Judith" (p. 349).

[85] See Enslin and Zeitlin, *Judith,* "Appendix I: Judith the Widow," 180-81. They point out that neither Jael, Deborah, the woman of Thebez (Judges 9:53), nor the wise woman of 2 Sam 20:14-22 are described as widows. They suggest that this detail may indicate a reflection of Alexandra, a woman idealized as Salome by the Pharisees, who ruled for nine years (78-69) as queen.

[86] On Judith's age, Enslin and Zeitlin suggest that the Maccabean revolt began in 168 B.C.E. and that the Hasmonean dynasty ended with the arrival of Pompey in Jerusalem in 63 B.C.E. Thus the dynasty lasted for a total of 105 years, which is the age assigned to Judith in 16:23. They use this data to support their argument that Judith's historical counterpart may have been Queen Alexandra, adding that Judith's summoning of the town officials is more understandable as an act performed by a royal woman (ibid., 181).

V

Faith and Literary Artistry
in the Book of Judith

The title of this chapter reverses the title of the dissertation. The substance of this chapter also inverts the general thrust of the other chapters. Whereas chapters I through IV are in the main descriptive statements about other studies of Judith, about the orientation and rules of this study, about the external design, and about the internal structural patterns in the Book of Judith, this chapter is in the main an interpretive statement about the meaning of the story and this study. Having completed a literary and rhetorical study of the Book of Judith, I find it fitting to return once again to the questions asked at the beginning of this dissertation: Who is Judith? And what do we know about the story which bears her name? What does a compositional study now permit us to say in answer to these questions?

Compositional analysis demonstrates that all sixteen chapters of the narrative fulfill important structural roles in the whole of an intricate two-part composition. This study shows that to excerpt a few verses or chapters from Part II about the deed of the woman Judith is to do violence to the whole of the story. To abbreviate the story by excluding or compressing the first chapters is to tell a story which differs in important ways from the one told by the author. Abbreviation makes the story into an heroic tale which is much easier than the full story. Part II, the tale of the woman Judith, entertains and even inspires us, but alone it does not confront us with hard choices. By watching Judith's model responses, we are somewhat distanced from the reality of the struggle involved in identifying the God of our own lives. The experience of the story is harder if first we agonize with the Israelites over the threat of the approaching enemy, reason with them as they try every way they know to get God's help, and finally come with them to the brink of apostasy. They decide that slavery is better than death, but they are not comfortable with their choice. It produces great depression (cf. 7:32). Their choice is one based on the conviction that they have no alternative.   Judith's emergence from the very midst of the community neutralizes their mistaken notion that they have no hope.   Her conviction that the God of Israel is a God free from human manipulation corrects and transforms their fear.   To avoid Part I of the Book of Judith is to miss the opportunity to learn what the people of Bethulia seemingly have learned about their God and about proper worship by the end of chapter 16. In the end, they have a triumphant song of praise to sing, but this comes only after considerable struggle.

CONVENTION VERSUS TRADITION

The Book of Judith can be understood as an exposition of the relation- ship of convention and tradition in the life of a faithful Jew.   In a day of hard choices, Part I teaches that devastation does not count and Part II that survival does not matter. Faith is loosed from its mooring of security in this story. Achior, not Judith, tells the story of God's special protection of the Jews. Judith demands that this story be let go, that God be free to protect or to destroy. Faith in this story involves neither magic nor quietism. It is a disarmingly simple kind of faith in the traditional God of Israel that is em- bodied by Judith.   Hers is the creator/redeemer God known in history. Judith proposes nothing that the psalmists had not already prescribed:

Let the high praises of God be in their throats,
and two-edged swords in their hands,
to wreak vengeance on the nations
and chastisements on the peoples.
(Ps 149:7-8)

In the story, Judith is the one who stands for maintaining "the old ways."   She wants to insure and preserve the continuance of authentic Yahweh worship. Yet in order to maintain the tradition, she is willing to do unconventional things.   Considered all together, her acts are almost un- speakable travesties of refined behavior. She tells the leading citizens of her community that they are dense-minded fools (cf. 8:14), and she makes a fool out of Holofernes (cf. 12:16-20). She does these things not for her own glory or gain, but that all—Jew and foreigner alike—know the power and supremacy of the God Yahweh.

The Book of Judith calls for a radical reorientation of religious sensi- bilities. Were Job to say to Judith as he said to Zophar, "Will you speak falsely for God, speak deceitfully for him?" (Job 13:7), Judith might respond that in certain circumstances such unexpected behavior might be justified.

Certainly on the occasion described in the story, she "lies" for the Lord. Her words to Holofernes can be understood in no other way.

In a sense, Judith is willing to break the law in order to maintain the greater principle for which it stands. But in no way is she a licentious person. Indeed, in the story no one is more disciplined or more faithful than she. Her community applauds her as "the exaltation of Jerusalem," "the great glory of Israel," and "the great pride of her nation" (15:9b). For Judith, piety is not rigid adherence to frozen modes of behavior. Yahweh, not ritualistic observances, occupies center place in her life. Pious rituals are means, not ends for her.

By lauding Judith, the community implicitly approves her deeds. The people find in Judith a model of freedom and courage. The last words of the book celebrate the fact that after her death no one spread terror among the people. Whereas Part I ends on a note of bleak depression with the people not at ease with the decision they have made to give God five days to act (7:32), Part II ends on a note of triumphant freedom (16:25). The real change in the story actually happens in the hearts of the members of the community. In the time sequence of the story, Judith appears publicly but briefly—four days in the Assyrian camp and a month plundering and celebrating the victory. Then she withdraws back to her roof-top solitude where she lives until her death at one hundred five years old (cf. 16:21ff.). The community find in her not a permanent leader but a way to acquire permanent freedom. She appears at a time when her people are between times, so to speak. They have made a decision to surrender, but not for five more days. They believe that they are lost, but she shows them an alternative. She is a sign of the ancient truth that by vocation they are a freed people, that they can choose life and freedom if they rely wholly upon their God. This, of course, is a message as old as the people of Israel.

For all the seriousness of its subject, the story of Judith is replete with light-hearted touches of comedy. That a woman as punctiliously pious as Judith does some of the things that she does, surely pokes fun at stodgy notions of propriety and proper religious behavior. And is it not high comedy to make Nebuchadnezzar an Assyrian and put him into an already destroyed capital city where he tells in detail his "secret" plan and gives an order to his chief general which the latter soundly disregards? The three-day, three hundred mile journey of the Assyrian forces, and the putting of sackcloth on everything in sight, including the cattle, must also be added to the list of humorous details. Surely Holofernes' four-day wait before trying to seduce Judith, his falling across the bed in a drunken stupor when finally he has his chance, and Judith's pausing to pray before chopping off his head are acts which satirize standard behavior in such settings. These and numerous other details and incidents suggest that comedy and satire are important dimensions of the Book of Judith.[1]

An adequate treatment of Judith as comedy or satire would require lengthy study. While this is not the place for such discussion, it is appropriate to raise as an issue meriting further study the question of humor as a conventional narrative technique in ancient story-telling.[2] Just as the architectural structure of the story is "classical" in the sense that it is patterned on repetitions characteristic of finely crafted biblical stories, so too humor of the type found in stories like Judith, Job,[3] Jonah,[4] Ruth,[5] Esther,[6] and Tobit[7] may share common characteristics. They all exhibit finely proportioned literary structures, they all have happy endings, and they indeed all use comic touches to provoke profound theological realizations. To be sure, in the Book of Judith humor is a potent tool used to describe unfolding dimensions of the relationship between Yahweh and the people of Israel.

---

[1]For helpful comments on parody and satire, see John A. Miles, "Laughing at the Bible: Jonah as Parody," *JQR* 65 (1975) 165-68. On the relationship of comedy and irony, see esp. Wayne C. Booth, *A Rhetoric of Irony* (Chicago: University of Chicago, 1975). On comic irony, see Edwin M. Good, *Irony in the Old Testament* (Philadelphia: Westminster, 1965) 14ff. Cf. also James G. Williams, "Comedy, Irony, Intercession: A Few Notes in Response," *Semeia* 7 (1977) 35-145.

[2]Comic elements involving (1) incongruity and irony and (2) a happy ending or resolution may regularly be set out in a carefully crafted story as explicit or implied or even artificial identities or antitheses. As we understand more about the architecture of ancient compositions, we may understand more about the structure of comedy or at least what functioned in ancient stories as "comedy."

[3]On Job as comedy, see J. William Whedbee, "The Comedy of Job," *Semeia* 7 (1977) 1-39.

[4]Cf. Good, *Irony in the Old Testament*, 39-55.

[5]Cf. Phyllis Trible, *God and the Rhetoric of Sexuality*, 166-99.

[6]Cf. Sandra Beth Berg, *The Book of Esther: Motifs, Themes and Structure* (SBLDS 44; Missoula: Scholars, 1979) for a study which by extension would lend itself to discussion of comedy as a literary technique.

[7]I know of no study which treats Tobit as comedy, though even a superficial consideration of the scene in which Tobit is blinded by bird droppings and the scene in which Sarah's father is out digging a grave for her new husband on the couple's wedding night suggest this story is a likely candidate for fruitful study as comedy. Incongruity and a happy ending most assuredly are present in the tale.

THE BOOK OF JUDITH AND THE JEWISH CULT

It is true that in the story of Judith, certain conventions are forced to give way so that new life can be breathed into the tradition. But it is equally true that later generations did not capitalize in a public way on the potential of this story. It is strange that a story so concerned with the language of prayer and proper liturgical observation never achieved a permanent place in the canon or a fixed day of remembrance in the liturgical calendar.[8]

Could it be that Judith is simply too radical a woman for the tradition to memorialize? The decision to exclude the book from the canon certainly points in this direction. The explanation that Achior's conversion forbade the inclusion of the book in the canon because of his nationality and because he was not first baptized is not wholly convincing. Is his joining of the community not comparable with that of Ruth? Deuteronomy 23:3 expressly forbade the admission of an Ammonite or a Moabite to the assembly of Yahweh. If Ruth the Moabite was permitted to join the community, should not Achior the Ammonite have had the same privilege? Enslin and Zeitlin point out that the sages reconciled this difficulty by declaring that the Pentateuchal law referred to males only, and thus only Achior was excluded from community membership.[9] This explanation rings of sophistry, and one wonders what motivated it. To accept the Book of Judith as a canonical book would be to judge the story holy and authoritative. And to judge the story of the woman Judith holy and authoritative could indeed have been deemed a dangerous precedent by the ancient sages.

Though Judith's story is set squarely within the framework of the tradition, its program is far from traditional. From the moment that Judith appears in the story until the moment of her death, she is faithful to the letter of the law but not restricted to traditional modes of behavior. Judith's fear of the Lord is so profound that she fears no one or thing other than Yahweh. Imagine what life would be like if women were free to chastise the leading men of their communities, if they dared to act independently in the face of traumas, if they refused to marry, and if they had money and servants of their own. Indeed if they, like Judith, hired women to manage

---

[8]Despite all its "model behavior," the story of Judith was never attached to a major Jewish feast in the same way that the story of Esther was attached to the Feast of Purim.

[9]Enslin and Zeitlin, *Judith*, 25.

their households, what would become of all the Eliezers of the world? I
suspect that the sages would have judged that their communities simply
could not bear too many women like Judith.

The special genius of this story is that it survived and grew in popularity despite its treatment at the hands of the establishment. The endur-
ance of the story testifies to the validity of the message that life need be
based on no security other than faith in Yahweh. Like Abraham, Judith goes
where she must go, though she goes with no promise of success. The quality
of the going is what seems to matter most in the story. The authenticity of
Judith's faith is incontestable, and her regard for her tradition unquestion-
able. Indeed on theological grounds—though not on historical or linguistic
grounds—the Book of Judith may have stood as good a chance as the Book of
Ruth of becoming part of the Hebrew canon had Judith been a male in this
story and had Achior been a female.

JUDITH AS A SECTARIAN DOCUMENT

The kind of lifestyle described in the Book of Judith, with its pietistic
emphases on prayer, devotion, and ritual, its veneration of the temple,
doctrine of determinism and free will,[10] and its orthodox adherence to the
Mosaic law, is often described as representing a Pharisaic point of view.[11]
Recently, Mantel has argued the case that the Book of Judith represents a
Sadducean centering of life on the Jerusalem Temple, not a Pharisaic centering on houses of study and synagogues, where Torah was central to the
life of the community.[12] His study hinges on the distinction that the temple
and sacrifice were the domain of the Sadducees, and most especially of their
most important representative, the Jerusalem high priest.[13]

Though I do not agree with Mantel's arguments, I will summarize here
the twelve key arguments he puts forward to support his claim that the Book
of Judith represents a Sadducean outlook as written from the point of view
of the Jerusalem high priest. In my opinion, his study represents a kind of
use of the biblical story in which fiction is forced to argue an historical
case. Because there are those times when a story struck in the realm of the

---

[10]Oesterly, *Apocrypha*,   175-76.

[11]See, e.g., Cowley, "Judith," 246; Oesterley, *Apocrypha*,   175;
Metzger, *Apocrypha*,   52; Brockington, *Apocrypha*,   46.

[12]Mantel, "Ancient Hasidim," 67f. I am indebted to Professor Moshe
Kennet of Kutztown College, Pennsylvania, for translating Mantel's article
from modern Hebrew to English for me.

[13]Ibid., 67.

imaginary does provide data about the factual stuff out of which it was constructed, Mantel's arguments merit careful consideration:

1.   That tithes were given to the levites in the Book of Judith indicates that the story was not written by a member of the high assembly or one of their followers, but rather that it came out of the circle of the high priests who were fighting to defend the rights of the levites to receive tithes from the people.[14]

2.   Judith's praying at the time of the offering of sacrifice and burning of the evening incense in Jerusalem probably points to priestly influence, since such matters were important to priests.[15]

3.   Judith's nightly ablution in the Assyrian camp before her prayers proves that the book represents a Sadducean orientation because this sect alone linked washing and prayer. Their strictness in washing the whole body for the purpose of prayer is based on the connection between the work of the heart and the work of the temple.[16]

4.   Judith's observance of the first of the month as a holiday from her usual fasting and prayer is a practice known otherwise only in the temple. This practice again witnesses that the book came from the circle of the Sadducean priests whose religiosity centered upon the temple.[17]

5.   The recognition in the story that it would be unlawful for the people of Israel to touch the ritual foods with their hands (cf. Jdt 11:13), is an indication of a concern appropriate to priests.[18]

6.   Judith, like the Sadducees, was careful to avoid eating the food of non-Jews.[19]

7.   The definition of sin in the Book of Judith is identical to that which most closely matches the definition appropriate to priests. Judith recognizes that worshiping of other gods was sin.[20]

8.   Though conversion was accepted by both Pharisees and Sadducees, Mantel argues that Achior's conversion, when considered in light of everything else, points to a Sadducean practice.[21]

---

[14]Ibid., 71.
[15]Ibid.
[16]Ibid., 72.
[17]Ibid.
[18]Ibid., 73.
[19]Ibid., 75.
[20]Ibid.
[21]Ibid., 77.

9.   Judith's membership in the tribe of Simeon shows that the rights of the fathers were important in this story. These rights were historically important to both Pharisees and Sadducees; but here again, were there a matter of dispute, the author would take the side of the Sadducees.[22]

10.   Judith's refusal to remarry is not disparaged in the book. While this would not fit with the Pharisaic ruling that women must be fruitful and multiply to show that they were created for a purpose, it does fit with the concerns of a priestly author. From the time of Ezekiel on, priests were enjoined not to marry widowed or divorced women (Ezek 44:22).[23]

11.   In the Book of Judith, it is written that God hears her prayers and that God is close to those who call upon him. In contradiction to what Josephus says about the Sadducees, here we have a description of their God as a personal God.[24]

12.   Judith acts as a prophet when she promises to tell Holofernes when the people of Israel have sinned. Only the Sadducees believed that prophecy continued after the days of Haggai, Malachi, and Zechariah, thus only a priestly author could have suggested that Judith could play the part of the prophet.[25]

Mantel's interpretation of the Book of Judith as a Sadducean document is but one of the sectarian options that could be argued for the book. While it would be difficult to make a serious case for Samaritan influence given the book's strong appreciation of Jerusalem, all the other sects that emerged in the post-exilic communities are alternatives.   For instance, Judith's militant murder of Holofernes might be interpreted as reflecting Zealot influence. She indeed had a passion for liberty based on the conviction that God alone was her leader and master.[26] Like a good Zealot, she seems not to have feared for her own life. On the other hand, like a good Essene, she lived a monastic-like existence, praying and fasting in her roof-top tent. Is the Book of Judith a proto-Essene document setting out a case for those, who like Judith, would choose to live apart from their communities, to observe the Sabbath with rigor, and to reject marriage?[27] Or is the book

---

[22]Ibid., 78.

[23]Ibid.

[24]Ibid., 79.

[25]Ibid., 80.

[26]Cf. Gowan's discussion of the Zealots in *Between the Testaments*, 201-8.

[27]Ibid., 211-32.

best understood as a Pharisaic document. Like a good Pharisee, Judith was involved with legal activism and faithful observance of ancestral traditions.[28] It is undeniable that the story of Judith places great emphasis on human responsibility. If scholarly consensus were to decide the sectarian alignment of the story, the Pharisaic position would unquestionably win.

The real problem is that we know very little about the divergent lifestyles that emerged in post-exilic Judaism. And we know virtually nothing about the author of the Book of Judith. Josephus does not mention Judith, and the Qumran documents have not produced even the smallest fragment of the book. Since the story itself is clearly an imaginative one, historical considerations of any kind are strained. Though Dancy can say that, "there is in fact no reason to doubt—though it is impossible to prove— that the book was written by an orthodox Pharisee,"[29] the text itself will not permit certainty. There is in fact no reason to believe that either a Sadducee, a Zealot, an Essene, or a Pharisee authored the story.

As a feminist, I have secretely hoped that study of the Book of Judith would bring us closer to recovering an appreciation of a mentality within ancient Israel that from time to time broke with patriarchy.[30] To put forward the case that the author was an ancient "feminist" would be as groundless as arguing that the author was a Pharisee or a Zealot, or a member of any other sect. I have not been disappointed with the story, but I would not want to argue that the author intended all the moments in the story which have given me pleasure. I am intrigued by the role which Judith plays in this story. She makes her own decisions in a man's world. As far as I know, only the Book of Ruth offers a parallel.[31] In both Ruth and Judith, women bind together with other women for mutual support. Ruth had Naomi, and Judith has her favorite maid. In time, we may recover the full meaning of these details. But for the present, these considerations permit only conjectures.

Theologically, the Book of Judith suggests a program to break any fetters which might bind or cramp the religious life of the people, be these internal or external constrictions. The story weds concern for Jerusalem with a return to Mosaic inspiration. The language of "by my hand" and of the

---

[28]On the Pharisees, see John Bowker, *Jesus and the Pharisees* (London: Cambridge University, 1973); Jacob Neusner, *From Politics to Piety: The Emergence of Pharisaic Judaism* (Englewood Cliffs: Prentice-Hall, 1973).

[29]Dancy, *The Shorter Books of the Apocrypha*, 71.

[30]Cf. Phyllis Trible, "Depatriarchalizing in Biblical Interpretation," *JAAR* 61 (1973) 30-48.

[31]Cf. Trible, *God and the Rhetoric of Sexuality*, esp. pp. 195-96.

triumphant song in chapter 16 seems modeled directly on sections of Exodus. In this sense, the Book of Judith is much like Josiah's reform of 622 B.C.E. The story advances the well-worn advice that the maintenance of the tradition insures the continued existence of the people. In spirit, the Book of Judith is closely aligned with the traditional ideals of a conservative yet innovative faith. An observant widow is a mother giving birth to a new vocation for all faithful followers of Yahweh—Jew and foreigner alike. To say her name "Judith"—literally "Jewess"—leads us finally to the paradox that all faithful members of the community have access to everything that made Judith great. To be like "Judith" is to carry within oneself all that is needed to break the bonds of fear that fetter the human heart and paralyze acknowledgment of the true God.

CONCLUDING REMARKS ON THE ARTISTRY OF JUDITH

Traditional modes of literary construction and innovative theological understandings mark both the form and the content of the Book of Judith. The story is structured along classical lines with repetition serving as its hallmark. Judith's appearance as a theologian and a warrior is surprising. She is a woman of remarkable freedom calling a people of remarkable cowardice to realize the potential difference between true and false reliance on God.

Compositional analysis of the Book of Judith enhances our perception of the artistic prowess of its anonymous author. It enables us, as Muilenburg would say, "to sit with this author and to think his thoughts with him."[32] Literary/rhetorical criticism proves itself a valuable tool in approaching imaginative literature of the sort represented by the Book of Judith. Knowing what is said safeguards theological interpretations that are true to the story.

Study of the texture of the two parts of the book puts to rest criticism of Part I and puts in balance attention to the deeds of the woman Judith. Study of this sort permits us to enter deeply into the literary consciousness of the narrative. The text itself has been the primary focus of the study. The data generated by this study are pertinent to an understanding of this text.

The exclusiveness of this interaction is both a strength and a weakness. There is no question of the value or legitimacy of this kind of study. However, there are many issues left unanswered and indeed untouched by a

---

[32]Muilenburg, "Form Criticism and Beyond," 7.

compositional study. The findings of a literary/rhetorical study must be put into the context of the findings of other branches of biblical criticism. But if this study has done its work, then we turn to the findings of others conscious in a deepened way of what the story itself has had to say.

We end open to new beginnings. An exchange between Judith and her favorite maid, or friend as she is called in the oratorio by Marion Verhaalen with libretto by Francis Rothluebber, invites us to enter into the story in ever new ways:

> Friend: Is your story told too easily, Judith?
>   The end too certain at the beginning?
>
> Judith: Friend, you do not understand.
>   You make too much of the ending.
>   My story is not in the end.
>   The story is in the going.
>   Let us return again to the beginning of the story.[33]

---

[33]Marion Verhaalen, *Judith: An Oratorio for Four Solo Voices and Chorus* (in press).

SELECTED BIBLIOGRAPHY

Books

Benham, W. Gurney. *Playing Cards*. London: Spring Books, n.d.

Bentzen, Aage. *Introduction to the Old Testament*. 2 vols.; Copenhagen: G. E. C. Gad, 1958.

Berg, Sandra Beth. *The Book of Esther: Motifs, Themes and Structure*. SBLDS 44; Missoula: Scholars, 1979.

Bettelheim, Bruno. *The Uses of Enchantment: The Meaning and Importance of Fairy Tales*. New York: Vintage, 1977.

Black, Edwin B. *Rhetorical Criticism: A Study in Method*. New York: Macmillan, 1965.

Booth, Wayne C. *A Rhetoric of Irony*. Chicago: University Press, 1975.

Bowker, John. *Jesus and the Pharisees*. London: Cambridge University, 1973.

Briggs, Charles Augustus. *Biblical Study: Its Principles, Methods and History*. New York: Scribner's 1891.

Bright, John. *A History of Israel*. Philadelphia: Westminster, 1972.

Brockington, L. H. *A Critical Introduction to the Apocrypha*. London: Duckworth, 1961.

Brunner, Gottfried. *Der Nabuchodonosor des Buches Judith: Beitrag zur Geschichte Israel nach dem Exil und des ersten Regierungsjahres Darius I*. Berlin: F. A. Günther & Son, 1959.

Chervin, Ronda, and Neill, Mary. *The Woman's Tale: A Journey of Inner Exploration*. New York: Seabury, 1980.

Cheyne, T. K. *Founders of Old Testament Criticism*. Jerusalem: Raritas, 1971.

Coffin, Tristram Potter. *The Female Hero in Folklore and Legend*. New York: Simon & Schuster, 1975.

Conroy, Charles. *Absalom Absalom! Narrative and Language in 2 Sam 13-20*. Rome: Biblical Institute, 1978.

Culley, Robert C. *Studies in the Structure of Hebrew Narrative*. Philadelphia: Fortress, 1976.

Dancy, J. C. *The Shorter Books of the Apocrypha*. Cambridge: University Press, 1972.

De Lange, Nicholas. *Apocrypha: Jewish Literature of the Hellenistic Age.*
New York: Viking, 1978.

Dentan, Robert C. *The Apocrypha, Bridge of the Testaments.* New York:
Seabury, 1964.

Driver, S. R. *An Introduction to the Literature of the Old Testament.* New
edition; New York: Scribner's, 1916.

Dubarle, A. M. *Judith: Formes et sens des diverses traditions.* Tome I:
Études. Tome II: *Textes.* Rome: Institut Biblique Pontifical,
1966.

Eissfeldt, Otto. *The Old Testament: An Introduction.* Trans. P. R. Ackroyd;
New York: Harper and Row, 1974.

Enslin, Morton S., and Zeitlin, Solomon. *The Book of Judith.* Leiden: E. J.
Brill, 1972.

Fishbane, Michael A. *Text and Texture: Close Readings of Selected Biblical
Texts.* New York: Schocken, 1979.

Fohrer, Georg. *Introduction to the Old Testament.* Trans. David E. Green;
New York: Abingdon, 1968.

Fokkelman, J. P. *Narrative Art in Genesis.* Assen/Amsterdam: Van
Gorcum, 1975.

Good, Edwin M. *Irony in the Old Testament.* Philadelphia: Westminster,
1965.

Gowan, Donald E. *Bridge Between the Testaments: A Reappraisal of Judaism from the Exile to the Birth of Christianity.* Pittsburgh: Pickwick, 1976.

Gray, George Buchanan. *The Forms of Hebrew Poetry.* London: Hodder and
Stoughton, 1915. Reprint edition with "Prolegomenon" by D. N.
Freedman; N.p.: Ktav, 1972.

Haag, Ernst. *Studien zum Buche Judith: Seine theologische Bedeutung und
literarische Eigenart.* Trier: Paulinus, 1963.

Hanhart, Robert, ed. *Iudith.* Vol. 8 of *Septuaginta.* Göttingen: Vandenhoeck
& Ruprecht, 1979.

_____. *Text und Textgeschichte des Buches Judith.* Göttingen: Van-
denhoeck & Ruprecht, 1979.

Herrmann, Siegfried. *A History of Israel in Old Testament Times.* Philadelphia: Fortress, 1975.

Kittel, Rudolf, ed. *Biblia Hebraica.* Stuttgart: Württembergische Bibelanstalt, 1966.

Koch, Klaus. *The Growth of the Biblical Tradition: The Form-Critical Method.* New York: Scribner's, 1969.

Lanham, Richard A. *A Handlist of Rhetorical Terms.* Berkeley: University of California, 1969.

Liddell, Henry George, and Scott, Robert. *A Greek-English Lexicon, with a Supplement.* Oxford: Clarendon, 1968.

Lowth, Robert. *Isaiah: A New Translation; with a Preliminary Dissertation, and Notes Critical, Philological, and Explanatory.* London: W. Baynes and Son, 1778.

_____. *Lectures on the Sacred Poetry of the Hebrews.* Trans. G. Gregory. New Edition with Notes by Calvin E. Stowe; Boston: Crocker & Brewster, 1829.

_____. *A Short Introduction to English Grammar 1762.* Reprinted in *English Linguistics 1500-1800.* Edited by R. C. Alston; Menston, England: Scolar, 1967.

Lundbom, Jack R. *Jeremiah: A Study in Ancient Hebrew Rhetoric.* SBLDS; Missoula: Scholars, 1975.

Memoirs of the Life and Writings of the Late Right Reverend Robert Lowth, D.D. London: W. Bent, 1787.

Metzger, Bruce M. *An Introduction to the Apocrypha.* New York: Oxford University, 1957.

Montague, George T. *The Books of Esther & Judith.* New York: Paulist, 1973.

Mowinckel, Sigmund. *The Psalms in Israel's Worship.* Vols. 1, 2; Trans. D. R. Ap-Thomas; New York: Abingdon, 1967.

Neuman, Erich. *Amor and Psyche.* Princeton University Press, 1971.

Neusner, Jacob. *From Politics to Piety: The Emergence of Pharisaic Judaism.* Englewood Cliffs: Prentice-Hall, 1973.

Oesterley, W. O. E. *The Books of the Apocrypha: Their Origin, Teaching and Contents.* New York: Fleming H. Revell, 1914.

_____. *An Introduction to the Books of the Apocrypha.* New York: Macmillan, 1935.

Patte, Daniel. *Structural Exegesis: From Theory to Practice.* Philadelphia: Fortress, 1978.

_____. *What is Structural Exegesis?* Philadephia: Fortress, 1976.

Pfeiffer, Robert H. *History of New Testament Times, With an Introduction to the Apocrypha.* New York: Harper & Brothers, 1949; reprint ed., Westport: Greenwood, 1976.

Polzin, Robert M. *Biblical Structuralism: Method and Subjectivity in the Study of Ancient Texts.* Philadelphia: Fortress/Scholars, 1977.

Propp, Vladimir, *Morphology of the Folktale.* 2 ed.; Austin: University of Texas, 1968.

Purdie, Edna. *The Story of Judith in German and English Literature.* Paris: Librairie Ancienne Honoré Champion, 1927.

Robinson, Theodore H. *The Poetry of the Old Testament.* London: Duckworth, 1947.

Rost, Leonhard. *Judaism Outside the Hebrew Canon: An Introduction to the Documents.* Trans. David E. Green; Nashville: Abingdon, 1976.

Ruskin, John. *Mornings in Florence: Being Simple Studies of Christian Art for English Travellers.* New York: John Wiley & Sons, 1877.

Scholes, Robert. *Structuralism in Literature: An Introduction.*   New Haven: Yale University, 1974.

Scott, Robert L. and Brock, Bernard L. *Methods of Rhetorical Criticism: A Twentieth Century Perspective.* New York: Harper & Row, 1972.

Steinmann, M. *Lecture de Judith.* Paris: J. Gabalda et Cie, 1953.

Stummer, Friedrich. *Geographie des Buches Judith.* Stuttgart: Kath. Bibel-Werk, 1947.

Thompson, Thomas L. *Introducing Biblical Literature: A More Fantastic Country.* Englewood Cliffs: Prentice-Hall, 1978.

Torrey, Charles Cutler. *The Apocryphal Literature: A Brief Introduction.* New Haven: Yale University, 1945.

Trible, Phyllis. *God and the Rhetoric of Sexuality.* Philadelphia: Fortress, 1978.

Verhaalen, Marion. *Judith: An Oratorio for Four Solo Voices and Chorus.* In press.

Von Franz, Louise. *The Feminine in Fairytales.* Zurich: Spring Publications, 1972.

Welleck, Rene, and Warren, Austin. *Theory of Literature.* 2nd ed.; New York: Harcourt, 1956.

Wittig, Susan, ed. *Structuralism: An Interdisciplinary Study.* Pittsburgh: Pickwick, 1975.

Articles

Alonso-Schökel, Luis. "Narrative Structures in the Book of Judith." In *Protocol Series of the Colloquies of the Center for Hermeneutical*

Studies in Hellenistic and Modern Culture. Edited by W. Wuellner. 11 (March 1974) 1-20.

Anderson, Bernhard W. "From Analysis to Synthesis: The Interpretation of Genesis 1-11." *JBL* 97 (1978) 23-29.

_____. "The New Frontier of Rhetorical Criticism: A Tribute to James Muilenburg." In *Rhetorical Criticism: Essays in Honor of James Muilenburg,* ix-xviii. Ed. Jared J. Jackson and Martin Kessler; Pittsburgh: Pickwick, 1974.

Baker, Aelred. "Parallelism: England's Contribution to Biblical Studies." *CBQ* 34 (1973) 429-440.

Ball, Ivan J. "Additions to a Bibliography of James Muilenburg's Writings." In *Rhetorical Criticism: Essays in Honor of James Muilenburg,* 258-259. Ed. Jared J. Jackson and Martin Kessler; Pittsburgh: Pickwick, 1974.

Bee, Ronald A. "A Study of Deuteronomy Based on Statistical Properties of the Text." *VT* 29 (1979) 1-22.

Berger, Robert W. "Ruben's 'Queen Tomyris with the Head of Cyrus.' " *Bulletin of the Museum of Fine Arts Boston* 77 (1979) 4-35.

Block, Jules R. "Fast Shuffle." *American Way* 12 (August 1979) 91-97.

Brown, Raymond E.; Fitzmyer, Joseph A.; and Murphy, Roland E., eds. "Editors' Preface" in *JBC,* xvii-xx. Englewood Cliffs: Prentice-Hall, 1968.

Bruns, J. Edgar. "The Genealogy of Judith." *CBQ* 18 (1956) 19-22.

Buss, Martin J., ed. "The Word as Embracing History and Structure." In *Encounter with the Text: Form and History in the Hebrew Bible,* 1-44. Philadelphia: Fortress, 1979.

Cowley, A. E. "The Book of Judith." In *The Apocrypha and Pseudepigrapha of the Old Testament,* Vol. 1: *Apocrypha,* 242-267. Ed. R. H. Charles; Oxford: Clarendon, 1913.

Craven, Toni. "Artistry and Faith in the Book of Judith." *Semeia* 8 (1977) 75-101.

Culley, Robert C. "Theme and Variations in Three Groups of OT Narratives." *Semeia* 3 (1975) 3-13.

Dresden, M. J. "Ecbatana." *IDB* 2.6-7. Ed. George Arthur Buttrick. New York: Abingdon, 1962.

_____. "Medea." *IDB* 3.320. Ed. George Arthur Buttrick. New York: Abingdon, 1962.

Dundes, Alan. "Comment on 'Narrative Structures in the Book of Judith.' " In *Protocol Series of the Colloquies of the Center for Hermeneutical Studies in Hellenistic and Modern Culture.* Ed. W. Wuellner; 11 (1974) 27-29.

Edwards, Richard. "Concordance for the Book of Judith." Alphabetic listing
    prepared from *Thesaurus Linguae Graecae*, 1979. (Computer print
    out.)

Encyclopaedia Judaica, s.v. "The Book of Judith in the Arts," by Bathja
    Bayer. 10:459-461.

Gaster, M. "Judith." In *Encyclopaedia Biblica*, 2642-2646. Ed. T. K.
    Cheyne; London: Adam and Charles Black, 1902.

_____. "An Unknown Hebrew Version of the History of Judith." *Pro-
    ceedings of the Society of Biblical Archaeology* 16 (1893-94) 156-
    163.

Gottwald, Norman K. "Sociological Method in the Study of Ancient Israel."
    In *Encounter with the Text: Form and History in the Hebrew Bible*,
    69-82. Ed. Martin J. Buss; Philadelphia: Fortress, 1979.

Hicks, R. Lansing. "A Bibliography of James Muilenburg's Writings." In
    Israel's Prophetic Heritage: Essays in Honor of James Muilenburg,
    233-242. Ed. Bernhard W. Anderson and Walter Harrelson; New
    York: Harper & Brothers, 1962.

Holladay, William L. "Review of *An Analytical Linguistic Concordance to
    the Book of Isaiah* (Yehuda T. Radday), *An Analytical Linguistic
    Key-Word-in-Context Concordance to the Books of Haggai, Zecha-
    riah, and Malachi* (Yehuda T. Radday), and *A Synoptic Concordance
    to Hosea, Amos, Micah* (Francis I. Andersen and A. Dean Forbes)."
    JBL 94 (1974) 596.

Jansen, H. Ludin. "La composition du Chant de Judith." *AcOr* 15 (1937) 63-
    71.

Jay, Ivan. "Additions to a Bibliography of James Muilenburg's Writings." In
    Rhetorical Criticism: Essays in Honor of James Muilenburg, 285-
    287. Ed. Jared J. Jackson and Martin Kessler; Pittsburgh: Pick-
    wick, 1974.

Kessler, Martin. "A Methodological Setting for Rhetorical Criticism."
    Semitics 4 (1974) 22-36.

_____. "Rhetorical Criticism of Genesis 7." In *Rhetorical Criticism:
    Essays in Honor of James Muilenburg*, 1-17. Ed. Jared J. Jackson
    and Martin Kessler; Pittsburgh: Pickwick, 1974.

Kikawada, Isaac M. "The Shape of Genesis 11:1-9." In *Rhetorical Criti-
    cism: Essays in Honor of James Muilenburg*, 18-32. Ed. Jared J.
    Jackson and Martin Kessler; Pittsburgh: Pickwick, 1974.

Krieger, Murray. "Contextualism and the Relegation of Rhetoric." In *The
    Play and Place of Criticism*, 165-176. Baltimore: Johns Hopkins,
    1967.

Löhr, M. "Das Buch Judith." In *Die Apocryphen und Pseudepigraphen des Alten Testaments,* 147-164. Ed. E. Kautzsch; Tübingen: J. C. B. Mohr, 1900.

McHardy, W. D. "Introduction to the Apocrypha." In *The New English Bible with the Apocrypha,* iii-v. Ed. Samuel Sandmel; New York: Oxford University, 1976.

Mantel, Hugo. חסידרת קדומה ("Ancient Hasidim"). *Studies in Judaism* (1976) 60-80.

Meleugin, Roy F. "Muilenburg, Form Criticism and Theological Exegesis." In *Encounter with the Text: Form and History in the Hebrew Bible,* 91-100. Ed. Martin J. Buss; Philadelphia: Fortress, 1979.

Miles, John A. "Laughing at the Bible: Jonah as Parody." *JQR* 65 (1975) 165-168.

Muilenburg, James. "Form Criticism and Beyond." *JBL* 88 (1969) 1-18.

_____. "Introduction." In Hermann Gunkel, *The Psalms,* iii-ix. Philadelphia: Fortress, 1967.

_____. "Introduction and Exegesis to Isaiah, Chapter 40-66." In *IB,* 5:381-773. Ed. George Arthur Buttrick; New York: Abingdon, 1956.

_____. "Is There a Biblical Theology?" *USQR* 12 (1957) 29-37.

_____. "A Liturgy on the Triumphs of Yahweh." In *Studia Biblica et Semitica: Theodoro Christiano Vriezen Dedicata,* 233-251. Ed. W. C. van Unnik and A. S. van der Woude; Wageningen: H. Veenman en Zonen, 1966.

_____. "A Study in Hebrew Rhetoric: Repetition and Style." VTSup 1 (1953) 97-111.

Murphy, Roland. "Form Critical Studies in the Song of Songs." *Int* 27 (1973) 413-422.

Nichols, Marie Hochmuth. "Rhetoric and Style." In *Patterns of Literary Style,* 130-143. Ed. Joseph Strelka; University Park: Pennsylvania State University, 1971.

Paul, Shalom. "Amos 1:3-2:3: A Concatenous Literary Pattern." *JBL* 80 (1961) 397-403.

Radday, Yehuda T. "Chiasm in Joshua, Judges and Others." *Linguistica Biblica* 3 (1973) 6-13.

Rideout, George. "Prose Compositional Techniques in the Succession Narrative (2 Sam 7, 9-20; 1 Kings 1-2)." Diss., Graduate Theological Union, 1971.

_____. "The Rape of Tamar: A Rhetorical Analysis of 2 Sam 13:1-22." In *Rhetorical Criticism: Essays in Honor of James Muilenburg*, 75-84. Ed. Jared J. Jackson and Martin Kessler; Pittsburgh: Pickwick, 1974.

Savage, Mary. "Literary Criticism and Biblical Studies: A Rhetorical Analysis of the Joseph Narrative." In *Scripture in Context: Essays on Comparative Method*, 79-100. Ed. Carl D. Evans, William W. Hallo, and John B. White; Pittsburgh: Pickwick, 1980.

Shumaker, Wayne. "Critique of Luis Alonso-Schökel on Judith." In *Protocol Series of Colloquies of the Center for Hermeneutical Studies in Hellenistic and Modern Culture*. Ed. W. Wuellner. 11 (1974) 30-33.

Skehan, Patrick W. "The Hand of Judith." *CBQ* 25 (1963) 94-109.

_____. "Review of A. M. Dubarle, O.P., *Judith: Formes et sens des diverses traditions*, Tome I: Etudes, Tome II, Textes." *CBQ* 28 (1966) 347-349.

_____. "Structure in Poems on Wisdom: Proverbs 8 and Sirach 24." *CBQ* 41 (1979) 365-379.

_____. "Why Leave Out Judith?" *CBQ* 24 (1962) 147-154.

Terrien, Samuel. "History of the Interpretation of the Bible." In *IB*, 1.127-141. Ed. George Arthur Buttrick; New York: Abingdon, 1952.

Trible, Phyllis. "Depatriarchalizing in Biblical Interpretation." *JAAR* 61 (1973) 30-48.

_____. "Wisdom Builds a Poem: The Architecture of Proverbs 1:20-33." *JBL* 94 (1975) 509-518.

Tucker, Gene M. "Comments on the Articles of Robert C. Culley and Burke O. Long." *Semeia* 3 (1975) 145-148.

Whedbee, J. William. "The Comedy of Job." *Semeia* 7 (1977) 1-39.

White, Hugh C. "Structural Analysis of the Old Testament Narrative." In *Encounter with the Text: Form and History in the Hebrew Bible*, 45-66. Ed. Martin J. Buss; Philadelphia: Fortress, 1979.

Williams, James G. "Comedy, Irony, Intercession: A Few Notes in Response." *Semeia* 7 (1977) 135-145.

Winter, P. "Book of Judith." In *IDB* 2.1023-1026. Ed. George Arthur Buttrick; New York: Abingdon, 1962.

Zeitlin, Solomon. "The Dead Sea Scrolls." *JQR* 47 (1957) 245-268.

INDEX OF AUTHORS

INDEX OF PASSAGES